# THE
# KOREAN CONFLICT

## SEARCH FOR UNIFICATION

**M.P. SRIVASTAVA,** D. Litt.

**Prentice Hall of India** Private Limited
New Delhi-110001
1982

**THE KOREAN CONFLICT: SEARCH FOR UNIFICATION**
by M.P. Srivastava

PRENTICE-HALL INTERNATIONAL, INC., Englewood Cliffs.
PRENTICE-HALL OF INDIA PRIVATE LIMITED, New Delhi.
PRENTICE-HALL INTERNATIONAL, INC., London.
PRENTICE-HALL OF AUSTRALIA, PTY. LTD., Sydney.
PRENTICE-HALL OF CANADA, INC., Toronto.
PRENTICE-HALL OF JAPAN, INC., Tokyo.
PRENTICE-HALL OF SOUTHEAST ASIA (PTE.) LTD., Singapore.
WHITEHALL BOOKS LIMITED, Wellington, New Zealand.

ISBN-0-87692-217-5

The export rights of this book are vested solely with the publisher.

First Printing                                              June, 1982
Second Printing                                         December, 1982

Phototypeset by Tej Press, Bahadurshah Zafar Marg, New Delhi-110 002,
Printed by Premodh Kapur at Raj Bandhu Industrial Co., New Delhi-110 064
and Published by Prentice-Hall of India Private Limited, M-97, Connaught
Circus, New Delhi-110 001.

# PREFACE

This work is in furtherance of my studies on Super Power Conflict and Foreign Policy Analysis, taking Korean Conflict as a case study.

The study of conflict, whether bilateral, regional or global and whether social, political, strategic or organisational, offers the most interesting aspect of behavioural exercises of comparative might, both diplomatic and strategic, on the part of the Super Powers in monopolising the process of development of international relations. While the political dynamics of a fertile local situation provide the nucleus for the beginning of a conflict, it immediately involves the Super Powers in the whole process of the management of the conflict, hard bargaining exercises during peacetime diplomacy and a liability for the ultimate resolution of the conflict, in accordance with their respective foreign policy interests. The Korean conflict offers one such example, among many others, in the post-World War II period.

In the Korean context, the interests of the three major powers, in the triangularity of their relationship, clash with each other. However, Chinese and US interests are identical in their common cause of containing the fast expanding and infiltrating designs of the Soviet Union on the one hand; on the other hand the Chinese and Soviet interests are identical in the continued survival of North Korea as a communist state and the ultimate communisation of the south—a policy which stands in contrast with the fundamental US foreign policy interests.

Besides, while there is a bitter rivalry between China and the Soviet Union, there is unanimity of opinion and identity in approach as far as the compromise formula of 'Federation' is concerned in the context of unification of Korea. On the question of support for the North Korean cause regarding the expulsion of American forces, while the Soviet Union openly attacks 'US imperialism' and insists on the withdrawal of

American forces as a precondition for any unification move, China, of late, is seen to be often cautious in supporting the North Korean stand on the one hand but often careful on the matter of the withdrawal of American forces from South Korea, on the other.

China seems to be more inclined in maintaining a status quo and even prefers a tripartite international conference as a first step to the process of resolution of the conflict.

Finally, I humbly express my deep gratitude to all those who have enlightened me with knowledgeable information as well as materials related to this project. It is with this help that the book is able to convey an objective view of the Korean conflict. I also express my gratitude to M/s Prentice-Hall of India Private Limited, New Delhi, who have accepted it for publication.

New Delhi                                          **M.P. Srivastava**

# CONTENTS

# THE KOREAN CONFLICT
## SEARCH FOR UNIFICATION

# CHAPTER I

# INTRODUCTION

## The Late Twentieth Century Approach to Socialism

The political and strategic aspects of the beginning and development of the Korean conflict are to be studied within the broad
framework of the confrontation between the two Super Powers, in
defence of their respective ideologies, more appropriately in the
power game of championing the cause of 'freedom and democracy' in
accordance with their foreign policy interests.

The possible avenue for peaceful unification may have to be
studied in the triangularity of relationship among the Soviet Union,
the United States and China with due regard to the nationalist
aspirations of the majority of the Korean people. However, within the
overall framework, the developing political and strategic balance and
counter-balance exercises in East and North-East Asia, under the
compulsions of the International Communist Movement, are very
relevant and significant to the study of the Korean conflict.

Before discussing the effect of these compulsions on the Korean
conflict, I would like to examine the fundamental mechanics of the
compulsions of the International Communist Movement in the galaxy
of individual interpretations in directing the course of the movement
in the late 20th century, in perspective.

Karl Marx propounded the significant theory of 'Dialectical
Materialism'. In his theory he peeped into certain fundamental forces,
which govern the process of the development of a society. Tremendous changes of far-reaching consequences have since taken place in
the mechanics of developmental strategy, which have led to create
doubts in the infallibility of the 'holy' doctrine in view of different
patterns of social and economic developments and shifts in values.

1

The great philosopher of the nineteenth century probably visualised the nineteenth century political, economic and social situations to continue for centuries altogether.

The scientific doctrine of 'Dialectical Materialism', propounded by Karl Marx in the 19th century, has been subject to varying interpretations by political philosophers and thinkers in accordance with the varying situations existing in different sections of society in different continents of the world. While the sanctity of the basic tenet has been the guiding-force behind all the successive interpretations, yet these interpretations have been put forward and practised under the compulsions of varying circumstances. The emergence of Trotskyism in Europe, Bolshevism and Leninism in Russia, Maoism in China, Euro-Communism, with Italian and French brands in emphasis, have all been motivated by the economic and social compulsions in local circumstances, putting emphasis on a correct interpretation of the original scientific doctrine. Just as the foreign policy of a nation is governed by the national interests of that nation, similarly individual interpretations of the original scientific doctrine have been put forward from time to time in accordance with the needs of the local circumstances and their compulsions.

However, in the Soviet Union, the Kremlin political philosophers and theoreticians have been interpreting the theoretical and applied aspects of the original doctrine. The concept of Leninism and Stalinism have long existed, but the latest one i.e. the "Brezhnev Doctrine" has modified the modus-operendi and the applied part of the 'holy' doctrine in accordance with the changed circumstances of the late 20th century. "Brezhnev Doctrine" rules that the Kremlin holds the responsibility of setting in order a fraternal house which is in disorder. The experiments in Czechoslovakia, Poland and Afghanistan stand in support of this new approach to the applied part of the 'holy' doctrine.

Although the "Brezhnev Doctrine" draws inspiration from the original scientific doctrine, yet it is a definite departure from the existing approaches and the fundamental convictions that had motivated Karl Marx to propound 'Dialectical Materialism'. This is due to the fact that in Communist Manifesto and in *Das Kapital,* Karl Marx has laid down the process of the revolution as a natural and a voluntary consequence of the exploitation by the capitalists of the proletariat. But the concept of a 'forced revolution', under contractual agreements or covert invitations or by means of forced armed occupation of a society, or by the custodians of the International Communist

Movement, is a definite departure from the tenets of the doctrine propounded by Karl Marx. This hybrid character of the Proletarian Revolution naturally suffers from contradictions and counter-revolutions and questions the very efficacy of the international character of the movement. Karl Marx had never emphasised the efflorescence of the International Communist Movement, based on armed occupation of one society by another or by seeking diplomatic 'invitation' by a big country from a small.

The thesis propounded by Karl Marx has been that the down-trodden people of the society, under the compulsions of the exploitation by the capitalists, will rise in revolt and will take over the means of production, will exterminate the capitalist concept and establish a government of the proletariat, working for the proletariat. Karl Marx also envisaged that the capitalists, who were few in number, would ultimately be defeated by the larger sections of the people consisting of the proletariat, the downtrodden and the exploited ones. Thus, the thesis of Karl Marx, exists on the very basic concept of the "will and aspirations of the majority of the people of a society", since ultimately the large majority of the people, consisting of the proletariat group, will triumph over the smallest section of the society i.e. the capitalist group. Unfortunately this due regard for the will and aspirations of largest majority of the people, as conceived by Karl Marx, is hardly visible in the late 20th century functional approach to the International Communist Movement based on the policies of forced armed occupation or seeking diplomatic 'invitation'.

The fundamental rules of human psychology and social psychology speak of the fact that the gene of resistance forms in existing contradictions in the dilapidated infrastructure of the society under the compulsions of suppression, chaos and confusion, and constitutes itself in polarity or multi-polarity, when the concept of leadership emerges; but the whole process is natural and voluntary and, in its sanctity, totally rules out any external intervention. However, in the event of any external intervention it becomes hybrid and disperses with contradictions and counter-revolutions. Thus forced communisation inhibits within itself the genes of counter-revolutions as has been evidenced by turn of events in Yugoslavia, Hungary, Czechoslovakia and Poland.

Thus on the basis of the fundamental principles of human and social psychology, an attitude of resistance develops in a state of sharp contradictions and communicates its expression in terms of reforms and is hardly inclined to accept violence. The developed economies of the world therefore do not warrant a change, particularly a change which is inclined towards totalitarianism. Similarly the touch of fundamental freedoms which an individual or a society has enjoyed, is the most significant aspect of a country with a developed economy, since such a country would aggressively oppose a system heading towards totalitarianism since it would clash with its fundamental values.

An important example of rift, among the leadership in the central politbureau, relates to the development, in first half of the 1960s, in the Chinese central leadership. The genesis of Cultural Revolution and the purge of leaders, during the Cultural Revolution, evidently confirms that a strong faction within the central and provincial leaderships had emerged and gained sufficient hold against party Chairman Mao and his supporters. The purge and branding of Liu Shao-chi and Lin Piao and hundreds of others as "careerists", "traitors" and "conspirators" by the Chinese press and publicity media stands in evidence that within the highly disciplined and security-tight Politbureau, the cult of "counter-revolution" and "factionalism" had not only germinated but led to an unprecedented struggle for power and existence, culminating in the launching of the "Cultural Revolution", when the "Counter-revolutionaries" were purged right from the head of state and Politbureau to the village levels. It is significant that while the rehabilitation of some of the purged leaders showed their indispensability, the bitter power-struggle, after the death of Chairman Mao, culminating in the public trial of the "Gang of Four" confirmed that even a highly disciplined totalitarian system suffered from certain fundamental inbuilt contradictions motivated towards a power-game.

The Chinese, however, in the event of extended application of the Brezhnev-Doctrine in the East Asian context may highlight through all press and publicity media and in the United Nations also, the usefulness of the hegemonic approach of the 'social imperialists'. Besides, the Chinese may also try to explore an opportunity for a conciliatory and pragmatic attitude, on the part of the Kremlin leaders, towards China, to help resolve the existing differences on equal footing and based on mutual self-respect and as equal co-partners in the International Communist Movement. Haldman's surprising disclosure of the proposed Soviet armed attack on Peking, if the United States could keep off the fence, may be considered by the Chinese as a conception of the present Kremlin leadership, and is probably still haunting them against any such future plans of the Kremlin leaders.

China, which has often been seen to consider South-East Asia as falling within her zone of influence and responsibility in championing the cause and providing a leadership to the communist movement, has been facing effective countermoves from the Soviet Union in terms of loyalty from the smaller states in South-East Asia. The Chinese attack on Vietnam and the continued conflict in Laos and Kampuchea stand in evidence of this assertion. The Chinese approach and policies have been under the compulsions of the division of zones for communist expansion within the broad framework of the International Communist Movement. The effective involvement of the Soviet Union in East Europe led the Chinese to determine their own zone i.e. South-East and East Asia to exercise their supreme power as well as control over the International Communist Movement in this region. This had been one of the important causes of the rift with the Soviet Union since the middle of the 1950s as well as a guiding force in the Chinese foreign policy, essentially after the Sino-Soviet conflict.

Reaction is a logical phenomenon in human attitude within the concept of suppression; and the suppression of human values under the pretext of 'social security' generates the forces of resistance, which give expression to pragmatic assessment of the utility of the existing policies in the larger interest of the society and the nation as a whole. The totalitarian concept is devoid of the free will and expression of the people and hence suffers with certain in-built contradictions. Besides, the compulsions of social security of a policing state help develop the exercises of suppression, which inadvertently helps develop an attitude of reaction.

The nature and extent of the rigorous and highly scientific propaganda, being carried out by the custodians of the International Communist Movement, by making fervent appeals to the people all over the world to rise in revolution, for the last several decades, evidently measures the nature and extent of the vacuum that exists between the 'holy' scientific doctrine, when it was propounded in the nineteenth century, and the realities of the situation in the society that exist today. In any of the two contradictory systems, the ultimate survival of either of the two systems will ultimately depend on the outcome, which is based fundamentally on the 'will' and 'aspirations' of the large majority of the people of the society, and not on sporadic contractual outbursts of violence or dissatisfaction by an almost insignificant small section of the people, deriving inspiration sometimes from across the border.

Afghanistan may cost the Russians the same amount of embarrassment as Vietnam has been to the Americans, and the continued embarrassment, in consolidating the communist hold around Kabul, may ultimately ensue a dialogue in the Politbureau on the wisdom of this costly operation. In the process of putting the blame it may ultimately result in a crisis of leadership coinciding with the fate of Stalin and Khrushchev. The traditions, laid down by Kremlin, after the Second World War, attest to this conclusion and speak of the contradictions existing within the 'big brother' family.

Thus the scientific Marxist doctrine of "Dialectical Materialism" has undergone flexible changes so as to be able to fit in the developing pattern of social, political and economic culture of the late twentieth century. The bare statistics of human prosperity in nations like West Germany and South Korea, with more than twice as much population as their communist counterparts can in no way be susceptible to the workers' revolution or the totalitarian culture.

Thus the concept of a 'revolution' exists or the creed of the 'revolution' breeds in a highly frustrated and much downtrodden society and becomes a subject of ridicule in a well developed society, with a higher standard of living, based on the so called system of 'capitalism'.

The examples of Hungary, Czechoslovakia and most recently of Poland evidence the existence of 'factionalism' and 'contradictions', among the nationalist leaderships, in the applied part of the dogmatic Marxist doctrine, within the framework of the International Communist Movement. It also confirms that a 'behavioural' and 'pragmatic' attitude does exist among the nationalist leaders, who wish to apply the Marxist-Leninist principles in accordance with the local situations, compulsions, requirements and priorities; and insist, even at the cost of being ousted from power, to adhere to their pragmatic orientation, instead of tuning themselves to the algebraic orchestral voice of Kremlin.

### North Korean Approach to Socialism

An investigative but academic exercise and a positive approach to the study of the Korean conflict offers ample opportunity to understand the theoretical and functional aspects of a self-characterised brand of Dialectical Materialism, full of innovations and motivations, in which a total deification of personality cult, dynastic-succession emphasis and a highly militarised social system are central points in the approach to the developing process. It is important to remember at the outset that the North Korean President Kim Il Sung, by following an equidistant policy towards China and Soviet Union, has exploited the Sino-Soviet conflict in successfully developing the 'personality cult' to the best of his advantage.

Within the broad framework of Marxist ideological commitment, the developing polycentrism, in the garb of resurgent Marxism, evidences a fundamental approach to the original 'scientific' doctrine i.e. to lay emphasis on idolising the leader as the only source of strength and fundamental truth for the people who are ruled by him. The leader is supposed to have derived inspiration from Karl Marx and transform it and pass it on to the people, who in turn are supposed to derive inspiration from the leader only orthodoxically. Although Karl Marx has emphatically stressed the supremacy of the Party, yet the Marxist-Leninist behaviour as developed in some places, puts the emphasis comparatively more on the Party leader than on the 'Party' itself. While the source of strength is the original Marxist doctrine, the late 20th century leaderships, in the galaxy of polycentrism, interpret the original doctrine in a fashion suitable to individual personality advocated in the overall interests of the state.

The balancing mechanism of President Kim Il Sung, in between the two conflicting communist powers in their theoretical and functional approaches for the fulfilment of the communist movement, found expression in his much emphasised 'theoretical' and 'revolutionary' concept known as the 'Juche Idea'. As explained earlier, every leader of a communist state, who could afford to make himself independent of Kremlin dictates, has attempted to add a little or to give a new interpretation to the original Marxist doctrine. President Kim Il Sung's 'Juche' idea is an offshoot and an evidence of Kremlin's somewhat loose grip on North Korea that he could afford to adopt an independent line, contrary to Kremlin's original dictates. The rise of Maoism in China, Titoism in Yugoslavia and Euro-Communism with Italian and French brands, and President Kim Il Sung's 'Juche Idea'—all fall in the same line. Whereas in the West European context, the motivation for the evolution of this resurgent Marxism has been more academic under local and circumstantial conditions; in the case of Maoism and 'Kim Il Sungism' or 'Jucheism', the focus has been on personification of the individual leader together with the concept of the basic 'scientific' doctrine of Dialectical Materialism.

Since 1945, the name, the early career and the 'brilliant' leadership of 'General' Kim Il Sung has been systematically and extensively idolised and publicised by using much adorned monarchical phrases like 'giant of history', 'beacon of hope', 'leader of miracle', 'legendary hero of our time', 'immortal', etc. For more than three and half decades, his personality cult has been reinforced, consolidated and escalated with a view to mythologise the 'almighty communist leader of the Korean people'.

An important motivation, on his part, to identify himself with the 'Korean Liberation' against the Japanese and to build himself as the sole leader of the Korean people, was the developing emphasis on the personality cult during the Stalin era. In the Soviet Union, the leadership of Generalissimo Stalin and the 'decisive role' of the Red Army in the victory of the Allied Nations, were emphatically and constantly highlighted and publicised. Besides, Maxism-Leninism interpreted and reoriented by Stalin himself was hailed as the only source of truth in Kremlin's ideological expressions. The Stalinist model of social, economic and political system was idolised and worshipped as fundamental truths of justice, freedom and progress. Thus Kim was probably tempted to emulate the Soviet personality cult in order to strengthen his own power base by intensively collectivising the central power in his own hands. This is how his personality cult developed and emulated.

Recently, in the process of deifying and idolising him, his birthplace, Mangyongdae, has been reportedly called 'the cradle of the Korean revolution', and his native house, even a tree, a small playground and a rock, associated with his childhood have been preserved as historical relics.[1] The village has been attracting many visitors, including a South Korean Red Cross delegation (probably a diplomatic one).

In the context of idolising the leader, it is significant that not only he himself but also the members of his family have reportedly been emulated as 'patriotic' and 'revolutionary'. His father Kim Hyong Jik, who is said to have studied in an American missionary school in Pyongyang, has been emulated as 'a pioneer and outstanding leader of the national liberation movement'. His mother, Mrs. Kang Pan Suk, is also emulated as 'the great mother of Korea and model of revolutionising women and the family'. An institute in the name of Kang Pan Suk has reportedly been founded in Mangyongdae for the commemoration of her revolutionary spirit. Even his grandfather is pictured as the earliest anti-American patriot and is reported to have led the battle for sinking the American 'private ship', General Sherman, which had sailed to Pyongyang in 1866[2]. Besides, the statues of Kim Chong Suk, his first wife and Kim Hyong Gwon, his uncle, have reportedly been erected with a view to commemorate their 'revolutionary patriotism' and their affection for Kim Il Sung[3]

The above informative exercises, meant for internal consumption, within the framework of Marxism-Leninism, are not only carried out by the internal press and publicity media but even full page paid advertisements in the USA and other countries, exhibiting a large size photograph of Kim Il Sung, are interpreted as evidences of popularity of the 'respected and beloved' leader in foreign countries, including the United States[4].

As was the case with Mao in China, similarly in North Korea, it is difficult to find a newspaper, a magazine, a song, a radio program, a file or a book without a direct or indirect reference to the personality of the President. He is frequently held as the 'father', 'the model for the people', the 'sun of the nation' and the 'most respected and beloved leader of the 40 million Korean people' (they include South Korean population also, although it is difficult to find a single photograph of his or any person praising him in South Korea).

These hyperbolic expressions and references made to heighten personality cult of the leader in North Korea are similar to those of Chinese expressions for Chairman Mao in the fifties, sixties and till his death in 1976. History shows that the development of a personality cult on these lines, supported by the concentration of power in a couple of hands, has led to the beginning and existence of a rival or opposed group, within the party hierarchy, smouldering in multiplied dimensions and waiting for an opportunity, which has invariably led to a power-struggle after the death of the deified leader. The most recent and probably the most appropriate instance, we have, is of China in the context of what happened to CCP sole deity Chairman Mao and his small coterie, which includes his third wife Chiang Ching, his son-in-law Yao Wen-Yuan, his (reported) son Hua Kuo-feng and Chang Chung-chiao, better known as 'The Gang of Four'. It is really very significant that the nature and extent of post-Mao decorations of Mao himself and the Gang of Four, in terms of not only the party's smouldering expressions, but in terms of popular expressions and support as well, that speaks of the consequence of a highly developed and adorned 'personality cult', particularly in a big communist country. It is more significant in the case of a neighbouring communist country like North Korea, where not only the North Korean leadership but the people also derive fundamental inspiration and motivation in political, strategic, economic and ethnic considerations from the Chinese.

From analytical point of view, it is very significant that the North Koreans have very close political strategic and ethnic bondage with the Chinese. In view of the nature and extent of their past association with the North Koreans, the Chinese will never accept any concept like 'Juche' from the North Korean leadership, in their mutual relationship—which they say has been 'cemented in blood'. From the point of political and academic analysis, the concept of 'Juche' looks 'insignificant' in view of the fact that North Korea still depends on China as much as it depended during 1950-53. And more important is the Chinese consciousness of their responsibilities and the patronage that they had and are still providing to North Korea. Chinese reaction to the concept of 'Juche' may be well understood by a recent example of their relationship with Vietnam. After the American withdrawal from Vietnam, Hanoi also tried to adopt a 'Juche' line in its foreign policy matters, and the subsequent lessons taught by the Chinese to Hanoi are well known to us. In view of Chinese behavioural patterns of relationship with small neighbouring communist states like Vietnam and North Korea, whom China has been constantly assisting in political, economic and strategic tasks, I don't think, China will have a mild attitude towards any such 'Juche line' or any kind of 'Kim Il Sungism', which may run in contradiction with the Chinese fundamental foreign policy interests. This is very significant, particularly in the North Korean context, since the Chinese face a major challenge from the Soviet Union, politically and strategically, in exercising control and command over North Korea.

Scholars have often argued about the real identity of Kim Il Sung and the opinion en masse goes that he adopted the new name of Il Sung in order to personify himself with the greatness and chivalry of the traditional legendary hero Kim Il Sung. The earliest Japanese police report of the military activities of a person named Kim Il Sung is May 1935.[5] This Japanese report names Kim as the leader of the Third Detachment, the First Company, the Second Army of the North-East People's Revolutionary Army, which was formed on September 19, 1933, as a Chinese Communist Guerilla Army.[6]

Kim continued his anti-Japanese guerilla activities during the thirties but with the beginning of the World War II and with the mounting Japanese offensive, Kim had to retreat inside Russian territory in 1941, and Kim himself has admitted that in 1941 his anti-Japanese guerilla campaign changed from a large unit open struggle to small unit underground activities.[7]

He returned to North Korea, in August 1945, after the Japanese surrender, with the name Kim Yung Hwan, instead of Kim Sung Joo and soon assumed the name Kim Il Sung. On October 14, 1945, he appeared at the Pyongyang City Welcoming Rally as 'General Kim Il Sung'.

The above short analytical discussion, on the controversies relating to Kim Il Sung's early career, has been made with a view to understand properly the 'personality cult' in nature and extent.

Keeping in view the mechanics of the propaganda campaign in a closed communist society, the exercises on eulogising Kim Il Sung's early career and family heroism may be exclusively meant for internal consumption in order to gradually prepare the masses of people to reconcile with and accept the high-tiding and overstepping emergence of the son—Kim Chong Il. Humble acceptance of the family tree and the acceptance of Chong Il as the 'sun of the future' has reportedly been considered as an outstanding qualification and an excellent performance of duties, even in industrial production and scientific research, for promotion among party cadres at all levels. Besides, to counterbalance the attitude of the senior and ageing cadres, the Politbureau membership has been increased from 15 to 34 at the Sixth Party Congress held in October 1980, with the induction of newly elected younger members totalling 11 and younger alternative members totalling 14.

Understandably, this exercise is motivated towards creating a stronger support and strengthening Kim Chong Il's power base in the Politbureau, like the 'Red Guard', in accelerating the decisive role of Kim Chong Il on policy formulation and implementation work; and in simultaneously proclaiming the Party's program and decision in favour of Kim Chong Il's succession as the leader of the State.

The original 'scientific' doctrine and even the manifold interpretations given to it, at time's interval, individual compulsions and circumstantial pressure—none of them either speak of or permit any hereditary or genealogical succession-concept in the decisions of the States; and thus it stands fundamentally in contrast with the basic tenets of Marxism-Leninism, in theory and in practice as well. It is difficult to find a parallel example having successfully resulted in its pragmatic orientation.

Of course, we have a recent example of a parallel attempt

made under the compulsion of dynastic motivations, and that is China. With the beginning of the Cultural Revolution and continuing purge of senior party cadres, including the Head of State Liu Shao-Chi and Teng Hsiao-ping and elimination of the most trusted but dissenting leader Lin Piao, we have witnessed a similar trend in emphasis on the part of Party Chairman Mao, to bring up his family members on senior positions in Politbureau and Standing Committee of the Politbureau, which included Mao's wife Chiang Ching and son-in-law Yao Wen-yuan.

China has obvious major political and strategic stakes, vis-a-vis the Soviet Union, in North Korea. Thus the question of succession to the head of state is a major policy decision, which involves major interests of the two giant communist states bordering and protecting North Korea.

Thus in view of their respective foreign policy interests, the succession question is an important question both for China and the Soviet Union politically as well as strategically. Moreover, the North Korean succession issue also involves the Chinese and Soviet comparative might in their respective championship of the so called International Communist Movement. Significantly, in the event of their interests being jeopardised both have shown their might to the neighbouring States—the Soviet Union on an invitation-oriented armed mobilisation and occupation of Afghanistan and China in their armed mobilisation in Vietnam and occupying some of Vietnamese territory as token of having exercised their supremacy on the foreign policy matters of a neighbouring communist State.

Now in view of these recent experiences of the two communist Super Powers, where does North Korea figure in realistic and behavioral relationship? Thus the whole complex issue of hereditary succession suffers from certain inbuilt and contradictory political and strategic considerations in the two communist powers' foreign policy interests in the regional context. In fact it is in this context that the current eulogising exercises for Kim Chong Il and the question of 'smooth' succession is to be understood.

North Korea is of equal concern for both China and the Soviet Union for political and strategic operations in the North-West Pacific and to protect their own sympathisers in northern Japan in furtherance of their own brand of International Communist Movement and specifically for the Chinese to keep an eye on the massive Soviet strategic presence around Vladivostok and the north Japan sea.

However, the question of succession, as the head of state, is a major decision in which the Chinese and the Soviet interests predominate President Kim Il Sung's personal interests either or North Korean national interests also, and thus the succession question of Kim Chong Il is to be understood having due regard to these predominating external considerations.

However, in the Chinese context, an important point for consideration is the Chinese developing pragmatic approach to the regional and international political situation in view of the detente with the United States which has been able to exercise some restraint or pressure on China and will continue to be a strong leverage in at least influencing the course of Chinese foreign policy in the decade of the 1980s and even after. It has been found that there becomes an immediate scope for cooperation between China and the United States at the moment their interests are identical on a given situation, whether it is an international forum or a regional bilateral offshoot. It is important to remember that the United States has got an important card in its hand which is of great diplomatic, political and much more strategic significance in balancing and counterbalancing the attitude of China and that is Taiwan. For China the identity of Taiwan is of much more strategic priority in its foreign policy agenda, and therefore in the East Asian and North-East Asian context the United States is also an important factor in balancing the attitude of China. Besides, Hong Kong is bound to emerge on the Chinese foreign policy scene with the beginning of the next decade.

Thus, besides its military bases, the United States has got an important diplomatic leverage in conditioning the attitude of China, and in the event of the oft-spoken 'power-struggle' or 'civil-war' in North Korea, on the question of hierarchical or dynastic succession, the United States may play an inadvertent role strictly in consonance with its own foreign policy interests. Now in such an event the United States sympathies with the South Korean Government are well known and the United States diplomatic pressure in balancing, to a certain extent, the Chinese attitude is well understood. It is becoming evident that the Soviet Union is getting more and more involved in the East European and the Persian Gulf region, and thus in the event of any leadership turmoil in North Korea, on the succession issue, the ultimate might possibly be decided by the Chinese. The Chinese may like to avail of somewhat U.S. leverage in support of their bitter antagonism against the Soviet Union.

Hence, in the event of a conflict on the succession issue whether dynastic or otherwise, the United States may possibly be called upon to play some kind of a role, and in this context the priority of the United States is well known and can be better understood in view of President Reagan's foreign policy statements. In adequate appreciation of some of these in-built cross-currents in the United States foreign policy, President Reagan's choice of an eminent academic and top expert on Korean affairs, Professor Richard Walker, as Ambassador to ROK, is significant.

It may be believed, in perspective, that President Reagan's administration is going to counter the Soviet Union more and more in East Europe, North Africa and the Middle-East, including the Persian Gulf both diplomatically and politically and much more strategically. It is significant to remember that in the East Asian context, the Soviet Union faces two Super Powers as No 1 enemies i.e. China and the United States, both ideologically and strategically.

Notwithstanding the fundamental differences between China and the United States in their basic attitude towards some of the conflicting situations in the East Asian region, there is a possibility of good amount of identity in their respective foreign policy approaches. And one general area of their common interests is to counter Soviet expansionism and strategic designs in East Asia. The detente between China and the United States and the Sino-Japanese treaty of peace and friendship are sufficient indications in the direction. Thus in the case of North Korea, having got involved in a power-struggle out of hereditary succession crisis, China, with the support of the United States, is going to play an important role in helping its own sympathisers to become the head of the state, against any possible move by the Soviet Union. Within the broad framework of its foreign policy interest the United States may possibly collaborate with the Chinese in finding out a liberal head of the North Korean State, with a precondition that the leader may open peaceful dialogue with South Korea, which may help create a possible and favourable environment in the realisation of the ultimate goal of peaceful national unification.

In view of the controlled press and absence of freedom of speech in a communist society, it is difficult to find individual instances of resistance to President Kim Il Sung and opposition to official policies among the junior and senior party cadres. Yet some instances in terms of 'uprooting counter-revolutionary ideological viruses', 'right and left opportunist ideas', 'insidious manoeuvres of hostile classes' etc. speak of the smouldering resistance among party cadres, particularly the senior party cadres.

There is a general consensus among scholars that Kim Il Sung, in furtherance of the ideology of a 'permanent' and 'uninterrupted' revolution, has been in constant search of his enemies within the Korean Workers Party and has availed every appropriate opportunity to purge his opponents. Professor Scalapino and Lee have emphasized that while Khrushchev attacked the cult of personality in his de-Stalinisation speech at the 20th Party Congress of the CPSU, Kim Il Sung adroitly capitalised on Khrushchev's de-Stalinisation move to work against Park Hun Yung's 'factionalists' in North Korea. Significantly, while in the Soviet Union the Stalin cult faced serious challenges, the Kim cult reached a new peak in North Korea, in 1953, by scapegoating the Park Group.

Although such rhetoric instances of uprooting the 'counter-revolutionaries' and 'revisionists' are common in communist ideological utterances, yet, in view of the recent Chinese experience, the existence of a counter group, as opposed to Kim Il Sung's policies, cannot be totally ruled out. Such a group may surface openly in the event of a power-struggle over the hereditary succession issue in spite of the fact that the North Korean Politbureau has been heavily enmassed with younger elements in support of Kim Chong Il.

Thus, in the final analysis, it may be understood that the beginning and gradual development of the political, ideological, diplomatic and strategic conflict between Soviet Union and China led to the beginning and proportionate development of an independent attitude of Kim Il Sung towards the two communist protecting powers, while simultaneously flirting with the two in order to gain more and more political support for himself and economic and strategic assistance for the North Korean State. In the development of his 'personality cult', he has very cleverly exploited the Sino-Soviet Conflict since neither China nor the Soviet Union wanted to offend him, that if one offended him, he would turn his back and become more friendly with the other. Interestingly enough, President Kim Il Sung himself has been particular in telling both China and the Soviet Union to consider such an eventuality and to memorise this lesson.

However, he has, of late, been trying to absorb his son, Kim Chong Il, within the political framework of his personality cult by boosting his image to the extent of naming him as his successor. Having joined the galaxy of Karl Marx, Engels and Lenin, interestingly enough he has become the 'sun of the nation' and his son as the 'sun of the future'. However it is important to remember that the candidature of Kim Chong Il, to succeed his father as head of state, is Kim Il Sung's own proposition and viewpoint. How far the candidature of Kim Chong Il is acceptable to both China and the Soviet Union, as a compromising candidate, is a question which has yet to be decided. It may be believed that both Soviet Union and China may individually apprehend the continuance of 'Juche' idea in the leadership of Kim Chong Il and may view it rather disadvantageous to their individual political and strategic interests.

President Kim Il Sung, being trusted and equidistant, has been able to gain reconciliation from both China and the Soviet Union as a compromise candidate but it may be too adventurous for both China and the Soviet Union to impose, on Kim Chong Il, a similar amount of confidence in view of their rival political and strategic interests.

# CHAPTER II

# THE BEGINNING OF THE CONFLICT

Korea, which had been under the Japanese rule since 1910, became independent as a result of the Second World War with the surrender of the Japanese in August 1945, after the atomic bomb devastated Hiroshima and Nagasaki.

The Allied Powers which had overlooked the question of an independent and unified Korea may be held basically responsible for the continued bitterness that followed after the bifurcation of the country. But the Allied Powers, after a prolonged war against Germany and Japan, were probably more particular about the fate of Europe than that of East of South-East Asia. Their satisfaction had been in the final victory over Germany and Japan and in sharing the loot, pending an appropriate decision, they could hardly visualise the impact of their temporary decisions on the future course of history and the nationalist sentiments of newly independent smaller nations. The power game following the Second World War caused unfortunate ravages in the destinies of smaller countries, which had to struggle for their existence following World War II. Korea is one such country, which is still struggling for its unification.

Though the Korean leaders of the time must be blamed to an extent for the division of the country, since the Korean independence movement, both at home and abroad, was ridden with serious internal disputes and a divided leadership having different temperaments, influences and ideological orientations, yet the partisan attitude and hasty decision of the Allied Powers cannot be overlooked and shares the major responsibility for the division of Korea. In view of their global priorities, in sharing suitably the loot after their victory and in view of their political and strategic requirements, Korea remained to the Allied Powers, a 'forgotten nation'.[8]

The Allied Powers, for the first time, concentrated on the Korean question in March 1943, when President Roosevelt of the United States met the British Foreign Secretary Anthony Eden. They discussed the post-war policies on Korea and Indo-China and agreed that Korea 'would fall under international trusteeship', and 'the trustees might be the United States, Soviet Union and China'.[9]

This idea of trusteeship in Korea came from President Roosevelt, who believed that the liberated Asian colonial states should be put under the great powers in order to have education and experience of democratic institutions. Roosevelt also advised this system to both Churchill and Chiang Kai-shek at Cairo, in November 1943, when he discussed the Asian affairs. At the Teheran Conference, the question of Korean trusteeship was once again taken up by the leaders of the three Allied Powers, Roosevelt, Churchill and Stalin. Stalin agreed to the suggestion at the conference.

The Korean question was also placed on the agenda of the Yalta Conference of the heads of the states from the United States, Soviet Union, and Great Britain in February, 1945. Here, again the American President suggested the idea of trusteeship for Korea, composed of American, Soviet and Chinese representatives. Stalin, however, disagreed with Roosevelt at Yalta and advocated an independent local government, President Roosevelt, however, insisted on his proposal and in support of his stand, sighted the Philippines' example and suggested, in case of Korea, the period of apprenticeship as twenty to thirty years. The one point on which both Roosevelt and Stalin agreed was that no foreign troops would be stationed in Korea, since this was in their own political and strategic interests. Meanwhile, Roosevelt died and the representatives of the two Super Powers agreed that for the time being, a four-power trusteeship comprising the America, Britain, Soviet Union, and China would pave the way for a future independent Korea.

Soon afterwards, the Potsdam conference dealt with the Far-Eastern question but the Korean issue was not discussed at this forum. Nevertheless the Potsdam declaration made on July 26, 1945, re-affirmed the early declaration, which held that Korea would be independent 'in due course'. The United States and Soviet officials had agreed at Potsdam, that after the entry of the Soviet Union into the pacific war, there would be a dividing line in Korea between the American and Soviet air and naval operations; but there was no discussion of zones for ground operations, since the

immediate landing of American and Soviet troops was not visualised at the time.

At this point the opinion of the United States Army General
George C. Marshall, is important. He did not visualise American
operations against Korea in the near future, but some of the indications given by him to Lieutenant-General John E. Hull, Chief of
Operations Division of the United States Army are significant.

The Japanese surrender in August, 1945, however, completely
changed the strategy of the Allied Powers. Now, the American
strategy changed from invasion to military occupation and disar-
mament of the enemy. The U.S. Ambassador, Edwin W. Paules
informed President Truman, on August 12, 1945, to seek agreements with the Soviets on reparation matters and suggested quick
action in the Far-East with a view to 'prevent Russian exercises'. He
also recommended that the United States occupy quickly 'as much
of the industrial areas of Korea and Manchuria as we can'. Ambassador Averell Harriman also suggested a similar action and suggested that the American troops accept surrender of the Japanese.
However, the United States instead decided to divide Korea at the
thirty-eighth parallel.

The decision relating to the military occupation of the country
and the division into zones was regarded as a temporary expedient,
in line with the decisions of the Cairo conference in December,
1943, that 'in due course Korea shall be free and independent'.
Following preliminary talks between the two governments, the
Korean question was discussed at the meeting of the Foreign Ministers of the United Kingdom, United States and Soviet Union in
Moscow in December 1945. The Foreign Ministers agreed to establish a Joint Commission consisting of the United States and Soviet
representatives to assist in the formation of a provisional Korean
government and proposed the negotiations of a trusteeship agreement. Following the announcement of these decisions, stoppages of
work were organised in Seoul, capital of the American Zone, and
street-brawls and rioting led to the imposition of curfew. The
United States Commander, General Hodge, told the Seoul press
that the decisions did not necessarily mean trusteeship.[10]

The American Ambassador's apprehensions, as reported to
President Truman, started coming true with the news of advancing
Soviet Troops at Woonggi, Chongjin, Nanam, Wonsan and the
nearby strategies in the North-East Korea. Now, the United States
government realised that the advancing Soviet troops may create a

strategic embarrassment for American interests in the region, and thus proposed that the Soviet Union, should accept the Japanese surrender north of the 38th parallel while the United States troops would accept the surrender, south of the line. The suggestion was accepted by the United Kingdo.n, Soviet Union and China. And accordingly, on September 2, 1945, at the time of formal surrender of the Japanese, General Mac-Arthur issued General Order No. 1, which provided for the acceptance of the surrender of Japanese forces north of the thirty-eighth parallel by the Soviet forces and south of it by the United States. With this order, the unfortunate division of Korea became final.

It has been suggested that the division of Korea at the thirty-eighth parallel was motivated by certain specific political objectives which included, (1) to prevent the occupation of the entire country by Soviet forces; (2) to place the United States in as strong a position as possible, to implement the promises of Korean independence; (3) to provide for the surrender of Japan to the United States forces; and (4) to limit the area of communist control.

However, the above arguments are disputable in view of interests of the two powers in the Far-East. Since the Soviet Union had been an important partner in the Allied Forces, it was difficult to overlook Soviet strategic interests in an area bordering the Soviet Union. Besides, the Soviet Union in view of her own political strategic considerations, had to assert its hands in East Asia after the Japanese had surrendered to the Allied Forces. The Soviet Union could not afford to sacrifice her strategic superiority with the United States where her forces had fought during the World War II, as Kremlin considered it a necessity to consolidate her post-war gains. The Americans therefore could not have afforded to take any unilateral decision on the territories occupied by Japan, after the surrender of the Japanese forces. This was also amply evident from the division of Germany.

In this context, the following interpretation is also significant; 'The two major wartime decisions on Korea made by the Allied Powers, the four-power Korean trusteeship and the division of Korea, became the wheel around which much future Korean history turned. As for the four-power trusteeship of Korea, it should be noted that the Allied Powers overlooked the possibility that the Korean people might resist, as they actually did, both because they had their own provisional government in exile and because they wished immediate independence. Particularly, the United States policy planners did not foresee the difficulty of implementing the four-power trusteeship with the close cooperation of the Soviet Union. As for the provision for acceptance of the surrender of Japanese forces, it should be indicated that the Allied Powers had a clearly defined agreement on the purpose and procedure of the occupation in order to limit future confusion in the political development of the Korean people, but hoped that war time cooperation with Moscow could be carried over into the post-war period. They erroneously thought that they could handle any issue that might arise during the military occupation of Korea.'[11]

However, the political decision of the Allied Forces dividing the country into two at the 38th parallel was resisted by the Korean people. They wanted and demanded a unified Korea and were against any sort of division of the country under the control of the Allied Powers as they felt that this would subjugate them again to one or the other Super Power. It is from this point that the struggle for unification of the country took an accelerated turn. The Japanese also, after their surrender, were of the opinion that such an arrangement may lead to an internal rebellion, as the Korean liberation movement, which was divided into several factions and had gained sufficient strongholds in and outside Korea. Also, once Japan had been defeated, it probably wanted an independent Korea, free from foreign invasion, in view of their own political and strategic interests. The Japanese also apprehended occupation of the northern part of the Peninsula by the Communist forces as an approaching threat of communism nearer to their own territories. Thus, the Japanese were against any Allied Powers strategic presence in the Korean Peninsula.

This action on the part of the nationalist leaders indicated their dedication and deep determination to achieve an independent and unified Korea. But there was division among the nationalist leaders themselves and Song Chin-U declared the formation of the Korean democratic party and supported the Korean provisional government in Chungking. Meanwhile, the United States forces had landed in Seoul and set up the United States Armed Military Government in Korea as the only lawful government south of the 38th parallel and dismissed the transitional government. The leaders of transitional government were recognised as members of a single opposition party and the new American administration in Korea appealed to the leaders of the Korean provisional government at Chungking to return to Seoul as private citizens not as officials of the provisional government. Syngman Rhee and a few others thus returned to Seoul as private citizens. It is evident that the lack of positive approach on the part of the Allied Powers created confusion and led to a chain of unfortunate events due to which the Korean people had to suffer and struggle for their independence.

Such arrangement, which was totally in disregard with the will and aspirations of the Korean people, was vehemently resisted by the Korean political leaders, who emphasised that a Korean Government, consisting of Korean people alone, should be established in Korea on the basis of General elections throughout the Korean Peninsula. The Nationalist leaders including the rightists and the leftists both declared that Korean provisional Government should be recognised as a transitional Government. A Central Conference for the Acceleration of Korean independence was formed under the Chairmanship of Syngman Rhee who, on November 2, declared that the Koreans could hold national elections on the basis of democratic principles within a period of one year after the recognition of the provisional government, and that the Koreans should 'refuse to accept joint trusteeship or any other measure short of independence'. Again there was a split among the Nationalist leaders, which weakened the national cause of independence and strengthened the United States policy of a Korean trusteeship. However, the Nationalist demand for general elections in the whole of the Korean Peninsula continued with a view to free the Koreans from American or Soviet domination.

To the north of the 38th parallel, the demands were continuing to embarrass the Soviet troops. A Committee for the Preparation of Korean Independence had been formed under the leadership of Cho Man-sik but it received direct transfer of power from the Japanese provincial governor. The Soviet occupation forces, however, exerted enough to eliminate the right wing nationalists from the Committee for Preparation of Korean Independence; and on August 26th, 1945, they created a Peoples Political Committee of Pyongyang Namdo Province under the leadership of General Chistiakov. Cho Man-sik was made Chairman and the Committee consisted of thirty-two elected members. On the pattern of this Committee, similar Peoples Political Committees were also created in the remaining three provinces in North Korea. The Political Office of the Soviet Occupation Forces led by Major General Romanyenko and his advisers controlled the Peoples Political Committees in the Provinces.

The Soviet Occupation Forces took quick action in establishing in North Korea, a government similar to that in the Soviet Union. Soviet Occupation Forces, on September 14, 1945, issued policy directives, in regard to the system of administration, which included (1) the early establishment of a government with the representation of the working people, industrial workers, peasants and the other Koreans opposed to the Japanese; (2) the distribution of land to the people engaged in cultivation; (3) putting the industry, which was under Japanese control, under the control of a Workers' Committee; (4) public control of all the educational and cultural institutions; and (5) the immediate purge of those Koreans, who had been pro-Japanese. It is significant here that these policy directives excluded the 'rightists', as the Communists had often alleged that they were Japanese collaborators. In this way, the section of people which was opposed to the communist policies, was excluded from power, and even Cho Man-sik was purged finally.

The Soviet authorities convened, on October 8, 1945, the temporary Five-Province Peoples Committee, which was later renamed as the Five-Province Administration Bureau. Cho Man-sik again became the head of this organisation. After two days, the conference on North Korean Five-Province Party Representatives and Enthusiasts was convened, which organised the North Korean branch of Communist Party; and it was here that Kim Il Sung then a major[12] in the Soviet Army, was elected the First Secretary of this branch. Thus, "the establishment of the North Korean branch of the Korean communist organisation, with those of Soviet oriented political groups acting as its core, meant that the Soviet Occupation Authority was ready to move following the Leninist principle of the supremacy of the party over the administrative organisation in the direction of weakening the North Korean indigenous political forces represented in the Five Province Administrative bureau".[13]

Thus with the beginning of the establishment of the communist regime in North Korea, under the control of the Soviet Union, Kim Il Sung gradually gained authority and established his position as the head of the government in North Korea.

With a view to re-considering the efficacy of the Allied Powers' post-war decisions on Korea, the foreign ministers of Great Britain, the Soviet Union and the United States met at Moscow in December, 1945, particularly to consider the modus-operandi of the Four Power Trusteeship for Korea. The Foreign Ministers' Meeting in Moscow, however, concluded with an agreement "on the creation of a unified administration for Korea as a prelude to the establishment of an independent Korean Government." The agreement, which came to be known as "Moscow Protocol on Korea", included four decisions:

1. that there was to be established a provisional Korean democratic government, which 'shall take all the necessary steps for the development of industry, agriculture and transport in Korea as well as the national culture of the Korean people.'

2. that a Joint American-Soviet Commission, representing the two commands in Korea, was to be established, and its primacy responsibilities were to assist in the formation of a provisional Korean government through consultation with the Korean democratic parties and social organisations.

3. that on the prospects of the Korean Provisional Government and democratic organisations, the commission was to work out measures for helping and assisting political, economic and social progress of the Korean people for the development of the national independence of Korea. The proposals of the four powers for the working out of a course concerning the four-power trusteeship for a period upto five years. These proposals of the Commission were to be submitted after the consultation with the Provisional Korean Government.

4. that a Joint Conference of the representatives of the Soviet and American occupation commands should be held within two weeks to consider urgent economic and administrative matters as well as the measures for some sort of permanent co-ordination.

The basic objective and the guiding spirit behind these diplomatic exercises of the Super Powers at Moscow were their determination to establish a free and independent Korea, as provided in the Cairo declaration of December, 1943, in due course of time, but the Korean people and their nationalist leaders were strongly opposed to any kind of Super Power domination over Korea for any period of time. Another important reason for a possible conflict between the two Super Powers was the mutually opposed ideologies and systems. It was considered difficult for the two Super Powers to get along in the difficult task of establishing peace in the Korean Peninsula because of the basic contradictions in their mutual interests and the conflicting modus-operandi in their respective approaches. Such apprehension proved true within the next few years with the North Korean attack on South Korea.

Added to this fire was the fuel of the ever-growing demands of the nationalist leaders for a free and independent Korea and the establishment of a government based on general elections expressing the free will and aspiration of the people. Thus, the Moscow agreement may be considered only as an academic exercise on the part of the Super Powers since the ever-increasing contradictions between them on various issues of post-war statements in Europe, were creating embarrassing and conflicting situation between them, under the compulsions of their ideologies and respective national Foreign Policy, which immediately involved the two Super Powers in a cold war lasting about a decade. Their academic approach in championing the cause of freedom and democracy in post-World War II conflicting situations in Asia, particularly in the Korean peninsula, as evident from their views at the Moscow conference was only illusionary since ultimately the conflict between the two opposite powers that they represented, culminated in a major rift between the two halves of Korea.

The Moscow agreement in December, 1945 was thus in total disregard of the will and aspirations of the Korean people, and in view of this, the Korean people rejected it and opposed it vehemently. While all the political parties had resisted it, the South Korean Communists, extended their support for the trusteeship with the argument that since the question of national unification was involved, they would like to cooperate with the allies. In North Korea also, while the communists supported the Moscow agreement, the Right Wing Nationalist leaders raised their voices against it and regarded it as "selling the country to the Soviet Union." The North Korean Communists, however, supported it with the arguments that the Moscow decision on Korea was the just decision in order to develop Korea democratically.

The Moscow agreement, however, once again surcharged the political atmosphere in Korea, as the leaders of the right and left wing continued to speak against and for it for quite some time. While the right wing leaders were raising their voices under the compulsions of their Nationalist and democratic sentiments, keeping due regard to the will and aspirations of the people; the left wing leaders in their full support to the agreement, were probably deriving inspirations from across the border in view of maintaining monolithic discipline under the direction of the Kremlin. The right wing nationalist leaders in Korea established a National Council for the Rapid Realisation of Korean Independence in February, 1946, under the leadership of Syngman Rhee and others in order to consolidate their strength in opposing the Moscow agreement on Korea.

Thus, once again, some sort of freedom struggle, for establishing a national government, with full sovereign rights, was again accelerated. The right wing leaders, overcoming their minor differences, once again united themselves and consolidated themselves to launch a struggle against any Super Power domination over the sovereign rights of the Korean people. In response, this led to some increase in the consolidation of their strength by leftists also as, in February 1946, about forty organisations, including the Korean Communist Party, in Seoul organized the Korean Democratic Peoples Front led by Woon Hyung Lyuh. In North Korea, however, the rightist leaders were put under house-arrest and accelerated efforts were made to fashion the North Korean administrative system in accordance with the Soviet Union. In a series of resolutions passed by the North Korean Communists, a desire was expressed to establish a strong socialist or communist regime in the North and to take over the South by various revolutionary norms. The Provisional People Committee for North Korea was established as North Korean Central Government, which replaced the five-province Administrative Bureau. The Provisional Peoples Committee established was consisting of 23 members, a five-member Presidium, ten departments, three Bureaus and a court. The Presidium, Peoples Committee was headed by Kim Il Sung as Chairman.

In spite of fierce opposition by the masses a Joint Commission was convened, in January 1946, in Seoul, which exhibited difference as in approach from the very first day of the meeting. The United States representative laid emphasis on discussing the 38th Parallel and a prompt administrative integration of the two zones, which was to be posed on a general agreement for a combined operation of transport, communications, a single currency and free flow of goods. On the contrary, the Soviet representatives emphasised on specific subjects like the exchange of northern electric power for the rice from the South, the exchange of certain commodities and equipment and the running of the rail and road traffic between the North and the South. However, the representatives of the two states, concluded the limited agreement, on February 5, 1946, which included, (1) movement of Korean citizens between the two zones, (2) exchange of mail, (3) rail, road, highway and maritime transport, (4) the establishment of liaison between the two zones to coordinate economic and administrative matters and (5) the subject of radio broadcasting frequencies. To sum up, this preliminary conference concluded that a Joint Commission of the United States and the Soviet Union should be established in order to facilitate the implementation of the Moscow Agreement on Korea.

After the above preliminary Conference, which was intended to discuss the Agenda of the Conference, the Joint Commission was convened in March 1946, in Seoul to discuss the implementation of the Moscow agreement. With the beginning of the Conference, the Soviet delegation demanded that the nationalist leaders, who had raised voices against the trusteeship, should be excluded from the deliberations of the Joint Commission so that the Commission could discuss the establishment of a Provisional Government for Korea.This was again a major setback to the nationalist forces representing the will and aspirations of the majority of the Korean people with the exclusion of the right wing leaders, from associating with the Commission. In view of this, the United States delegation suggested that the representatives of the Korean people should at least be permitted to express their views on any subject if they so wish. Thus, a long discussion on the question of the Association of Korean Peoples representatives with the deliberations of the Commission. Afterwards, the Soviet delegation informed the American delegation that they have received instructions from higher authorities to stop the work and return to North Korea and thus after 24 sittings from March 20 to May 6, 1946, the Joint Commission was adjourned on May 8, 1946.

The adjournment of the Joint Commission followed planned and calculated attempts on the part of the Soviet Union to streamline the administration, consolidation of power and the organisation of the Communist Party in North Korea with a view to establish their complete hold over the North Korea. This was another significant step in North Korea after the Communist takeover, in the direction of complete communisation of North Korea. The Korean Communist Party, which was divided into two parties i.e. the North Korean Communist Party with Kim Il Sung as its Chairman and the New Democratic Party, with Kim Tu-bong as its Chairman, was combined into one, the North Korean Workers Party (Puk Choson Rodong Tang) on August 29, 1946. Kim Tu-bong was elected the Chairman of the new party and Kim Il Sung as Vice-Chairman. This led to the holding of general elections in North Korea, on

November 3, 1946, to elect the members of the province, city, country and the District Peoples Committee. The North Korean Supreme Peoples Assembly was inaugurated on February 17, 1947, as the highest legislative body in the North. A new eleven-member Presidium was created, which was headed by Kim Il Sung. A new twenty-two-member Central Peoples Committee was also created, which was headed by Kim Il Sung, which consisted of several ministries and bureaux. Thus, North Korea established a new system of government strictly on communist pattern.

In South Korea, the American Military Government took a decision to establish the South Korean interim Legislative Assembly, which would supercede the Representative Democratic Council. It was proposed that half of the 90 members of the Legislative Assembly were to be elected and half of them were to be nominated. This decision of the American Military Government met with the stiff resistance from the South Korean Nationalist leaders and led to the beginning of a power struggle in South Korea. While the rightist leaders agitated for the establishment of a separate independent state, the leftist leaders bitterly criticised and opposed the American decision alleging that the American policy was intended to separate the 2 halves of Korea. The American Military Government, however, tried to control these counter-activities and the attempts included the closer of the left-wing newspapers, the arrest of many prominent Communist leaders and a few other measures. However, the activities of the Communist leaders continued to escalate. In response to these political activities, the United States Administration declared that the concept of a four-power trusteeship was the only reasonable approach in the process of the unification of Korea. This again led to an outburst from the nationalist leaders and the communists which included an attempt by the former Korean Provisional Government to declare itself in March 1947, the de facto government of the country. This led to another outburst with the left-wing demonstrations, which denounced the American decisions as well as the rightist moves, resulting in the arrest of thousands of communist leaders in South Korea.

In view of these developments, General Hodge reported to Washington that immediate measures for the unification of Korea should be taken, in view of an imminent 'civil war'. Thus, on the initiative of the United States, it was decided to resume the meeting of the Joint Commission, on May 21, 1947. The Joint Communique, which was issued on June 12, 1947, outlined a compromising method for consultation. But soon a conflict over acquisitions started between the Soviet and American delegates, which nullified the progress of any negotiations. However, in order to overcome the deadlock, the United States Acting Secretary of State Robert A. Lovett sent a new proposal to the Foreign Ministers of Soviet Union, China and the United Kingdom. He proposed a conference in Washington in September, 1947, to find out a workable substitute for the Moscow Agreement and emphasised on holding the elections in Korea under the supervision of the United Nations, in the process of establishing a provisional responsible legislature and government. While the United Kingdom and China accepted the United States proposal, the Soviet Union rejected it. The Soviet view was that such a conference would be outside the scope of the Moscow Agreement. Yet, the United States decided to discuss the Korean question in the forthcoming United Nations General Assembly.

The proposal was included in the United Nations General Assembly agenda despite the opposition of the Soviet Union and the communist bloc. When the Korean question came up for discussion in the General Assembly, it decided by a vote of 41 to 6 with 7 abstentions, to adopt the recommendations of the Joint Committee and referred the Korean question to the First Committee for consideration and report. In response, however, the Soviet Union sharply reacted and demanded the withdrawal of all foreign troops from Korea and to allow the Koreans to organise a self-government without any outside interference. This demand was put forward by the Soviet Union delegations to the Joint Commission in Seoul, but the United States delegation rejected it, as this was a question outside the functions and responsibilities of the Joint Commission. It is significant that the Soviet proposal of the withdrawal of foreign troops from Korea excited South Korean rightists, who themselves had once demanded the withdrawal of foreign troops and the holding of free general elections in the process of the establishment of a self-government in Korea. Any attempt on the withdrawal of American forces from South Korea was only meant to boost the morale of the northern communist forces to run over the South. So the southern rightists including Syngman Rhee advocated the continuance of American troops in South Korea. The United States submitted a draft resolution on October 17, in the First Committee of the General Assembly, which provided for the holding of elections under the supervision of the occupying powers in their respective zones by March 31, 1948. The draft resolution also provided the creation of a National Assembly and a national government under the observations of United Nations Commission; and the new National Government may settle the question of the withdrawal of foreign forces with the occupying powers. It also held that the representation to the National Assembly was to be made on the basis of the population which meant that South Korea, with 2/3rd population would get about 2/3rd representation.

When the deliberations of the First Committee began on October 28, 1947, the American delegates emphasised on the above points but Soviet delegates contended that a responsible government could not be established in Korea, without a complete withdrawal of foreign troops. The Soviet delegates, submitted their own draft resolution, which proposed that the General Assembly should recommend to the United States and the U.S.S.R. the simultaneous withdrawal of their troops from South and North Korea with the beginning of 1948 and thus, to create an atmosphere, which may enable the Korean people to establish their own self-government. The Soviet delegates also proposed that the participation of the Korean people in the settlement of the Korean question was a necessity, and thus the First Committee should also invite the representatives of the Korean peoples to enable them to express their views. The United States representatives dismissed this contention on the ground that, such an attempt of including the representative of the people, in joint discussions, had earlier proved to be futile and thus, the United States delegates suggested that a United Nations Temporary Commission on Korea should be established to facilitate and expedite the question of participating elected Korean representatives.

The First Committee, which met on October 30, 1947, finally rejected the Soviet proposal by a vote of 35 to 6 with 10 abstentions, and accepted the American amendment by a vote of 41 to zero with 7 abstentions. Thus, the resolution recommended by the First Committee provided for a Temporary Commission on Korea, which would consist of the representatives of China, Canada, Australia, India, France, Philippines, Syria, Ukraina and El Salvador. The activities of the Commission were prescribed as to observe elections to advise elected Korean representatives for the establishment of a National Government and also to advise the National Government to make necessary arrangements for Korean independence. Accordingly, the elections were to be held before March 31, 1948, on the basis of adult suffrage and secret ballot.

However, when the United Nations Temporary Commission on Korea started functioning and send letters of introduction to the Military Commanders in both the zones, it met with major difficulties as the Soviet Commander on the northern side refused to accept the letter of introduction. The United Nations Temporary Commission on Korea referred the question to the Interim Committee of the General Assembly, which considered the question on February 19, 1948. Before the Committee, the American view was that in the existing conditions, if it was difficult to hold general elections throughout Korea, then the United Nations may hold the elections in South Korea only, so that a beginning for the establishment of a responsible government, may be made, and submitted these opinions in a draft resolution. This draft resolution, however, raised a controversy among the American allies themselves, as they argued that in the event of holding elections in South Korea alone, it may result in a permanent division of the country, and which would inadvertently be understood as giving recognition to the North Korean government. Notwithstanding, the American draft resolution was approved on February 26, 1948 by a vote of 31 to 2 with 11 abstentions, and thus, the UNTCOK decided to proceed on implementing it.

This controversy was likely to cast its due impact on the political leaders belonging to different political parties having different political attitudes. While Syngman Rhee supported the United Nations resolution, since he and his National Council for Rapid Realisation of Korean Independence strongly felt that a strong National Government in the South was a pre-requisite in defending South Korea from any northern designs. But the communists strongly opposed the UNTCOK decision for separate elections in South Korea and they suggested that a meeting of the political leaders from North and South should be called, with a view to discuss the political situation in the North and South, and the withdrawal of foreign troops from Korea. Their activities led to riots and violence and strikes. Some influential and moderate leaders of the South united themselves, believedly on motivations from the North, and suggested that a South North Political Consultation Conference should be held to work out the establishment of a democratic state in the Korean peninsula. However, their proposal was accepted by the North Korean Workers Party as well as by other erstwhile political parties in the North. The meeting, held on April 19, 1948, in North Korea, was attended by 695 delegates from the South and North. In the meeting, the proposals of the North Korean Communists were approved and a Joint Communique was issued, on April 30, 1948, which expressed opposition to separate elections in the South, and reiterated on the withdrawal of foreign troops, and also proposed to hold an all-Korean political conference in order to establish a provisional government. It was said that a National Government, established in this way, will arrange to hold national elections in the North and South for the establishment of a Constituent Assembly, which would draft a constitution for a unified Korean government.

However, the above deliberations and resolutions were looked into by the South Korean leaders as a purely communist design to 'secure hegemony over all of Korea', and thus they disapproved these decisions. The emphasis on the withdrawal of foreign troops from Korea also alarmed the South Koreans since in the absence of American troops, they more or less felt insecure, in view of the communist attitude of communising the Korean peninsula.

In South Korea, the General elections were held on May 10, 1948 to elect members to the National Assembly in accordance with the United Nations resolution. These were the first general elections in which 95.5% of the total registered voters and 75% of all eligible voters voted. When the results were declared, the rightists had captured almost half of the 198 elected members. None of the Assembly members was registered as a communist, although 59 out of 85 independents had leftist leanings, and the remaining 35 were moderate rightists. Accordingly, the National Assembly was convened on May 31, the Constitution was adopted on July 12 and Syngman Rhee was elected the first President of the new government on July 20, 1948. The new Republic of Korea was formally inaugurated in Seoul on August 15, 1948. The United States, soon accorded the recognition to the new government and the American military administration in Korea came to an end.

However, the establishment of a responsible government in South, on the basis of free will and aspirations of the people, passed enough ladders in the whole of the Communist world, particularly the Soviet Union and North Korea. In response and deterrence attempts were made to strengthen the communist type of administrative system in the North to prevent the impact of the democratic wave from the South in the minds of the North Korean people.

The unfortunate division of Korea led to a chain of events, which compelled the Koreans South of the 38th parallel to guard against their brethren north of the parallel and thus an era of unprecedented mistrust and suspicion between the peoples of one land. This may be called a legacy of the indecisiveness on the part of the Allied Powers in total disregard of the independence and freewill of the Korean people. The beginning of the communist involvement in North Korea, with the division of the 38th parallel gradually led to the Pyongyang regime's armed attack on the South in 1950.

# THE CULMINATION OF THE CONFLICT

The political situation that developed in the Korean Peninsula, after the Korean armistice agreement, contained within itself seeds of conflicting avenues and assertions in terms of political attitudes and exercises. After liberation, while on the part of the people of Korea, it was a pathetic expression for independence and self-government, which was extremely political, but on the part of the Super Powers, it was wholly strategic. The Korean people wanted peace and stability after being liberated from the Japanese colonial rule and aspired for a free and democratic state. Neither the southern, nor the northern people wanted a divided country or any sort of dictatorial rule. A country which had been under colonial rule for several decades was bound to suffer some sort of confusion soon after independence but this by no means gave a licence to the Super Powers to deal with Korea the way they wanted to and change the course of her destiny to suit their own strategic interest, under the guise of helping to put the country in order after her liberation.

The custodians of 'democracy and free will' failed in their duty to the country they helped liberate from the yoke of foreign rule.

The compulsion of the International Communist Movement was also responsible for the unfortunate political and strategic situation that followed on the Korean peninsula after the liberation of the country from Japanese rule. The Soviet Union, which helped the Allies to defeat Japan, had its own strategic needs of expansion of communism. During World War II, a state of confusion prevailed and the Soviet Union claimed as much territory as possible in the East and the West for establishing its own satellite states. These compulsions then motivated the Soviets to occupy the northern part of the country as a suitable interim formula, soon after the defeat of

Japan. But the American and British defence and foreign policy planners, at the time, did not realise that any concessions given to the Soviet Union would mean the extension of Marxist ideology and the establishment of Kremlin proto-type states. Even after the end of the Japanese rule in Korea, the idea of trusteeship could easily have been abandoned by a majority decision of the Allied Powers and the unfortunate developments on the Korean peninsula could have been easily avoided. In this way, a unified and powerful Korea could have worked as a bulwark against communist expansion in the Far-East. But probably the global strategic priorities of the United States, Britain and France, which concentrated mainly on the security of the European states, compelled them to overlook the fate of the East Asian and South East Asian states. The political and strategic confusion, that followed after the World War II in East Asia and South East Asia, is to be blamed to the Super Powers' recalcitrant attitude in settling these affairs in a just and logical way. Thus, hurriedly Korea was divided into two at the 38th parallel and Vietnam at the 17th parallel. What happened to these two countries has been an obvious example of the compromise reached between the big powers in settling the fate of these countries.

The multi-polarity in the political attitude of the Korean people after their liberation was in accordance with the fundamental logic of a developing society, heading for a self-governed democratic rule. Similarly, the 'factionalism' and 'opportunism', on the part of some of the leaders in the North and South, was a necessary ingredient for the breeding of the democratic process heading towards polarisation and a concensus stage in determining their own future in the best interest of the country. The leftist faction, which has always and everywhere derived inspirations from across the border, needed effective counter-measures to contain nationalist political and strategic activities. 'Socialist imperialism', which is the 20th century term for the 19th century form of imperialism is openly infiltrating the free societies under the new garb of Kremlin led 'proletarian internationalism'. The sympathisers of proletarian internationalism, derive inspiration from across the border and counter the forces of freedom and democracy. A similar situation existed on the Korean peninsula after the Second World War, where the communists aspired a Moscow proto-type government.

The origin of the Korean War is to be traced in the dilapidated political and strategic infrastructure of Korea and the Imperialist desires of the Soviet Union and China after the World War II within the framework of the International Communist Movement. Soviet Union, having established her control over the East European states as well as completed the process of communisation in that part of the world and in China, probably planned for further infiltration and consolidation in East Asia. The Korean peninsula, where it had already established control in the north, was taken as a challenging target. On the other hand, China too after the 1949 revolution aspired to complete the process of expansion in the geographical mainland by over-running South Korea. Japan, which had completely surrendered, was not considered strong enough to resist communist expansion in the East. The United States was already pre-occupied with the security and, management of the West European post-war problems and hence was not thought likely to enter into a war in East Asia with the Soviet Union. These were the primary motivations for the communist forces of Soviet Union and China to help the northern communist forces launch an attack on the south in 1950.

The years following the Second World War were the years of confusion for the newly liberated under-developed and developing countries because of the immediate post-liberation problems. And the state of chaos and confusion anywhere in the world becomes the most opportune time for the communists to escalate their activities, create more confusion and chaos and finally provoke violence calling it a 'revolution' and then establish a so-called government of the 'workers and peasants'.

A similar situation existed on the Korean peninsula in the aftermath of the Second World War and communists from within the country and outside, were involved in their behavioural mechanics in North and South Korea. However, they had the advantage of having two communist giant neighbours, China and the Soviet Union, making strategic assistance from those available at any moment. Thus geographically, whether on land, sea or in air, the Korean peninsula was an easy target for China and Soviet Union to launch an armed attack strategically. Thus, the expansion of communist ideologies in the whole of the Korean peninsula fell within the ideology and responsibilities and strategic targets of China and Soviet Union. It became an immediate priority within the concept of their dogmatic imperialist framework.

Professor Kim Chum-kon rightly observes that Russian occupation policy in North Korea and subsequent assistance programs were geared in part to creating bases in North Korea for use in expanding its interests and ideological influence elsewhere in the Far East. Accordingly, North Korea assumed the nature, from the outset of a proxy of the Soviet Union, which ruled North Korea to serve the goals and national interests of the Soviet Union. The fact is that Kim Il Sung and other communists in power in North Korea were mostly those who were invited to Moscow for political training during World War II. This, however, substantiates the theory of proxy rule. The Russians let their proxies to coerce and control the party, People's Committees and armed forces of North Korea with the threat of violence, and thereby subsumed the region of North Korea into the Soviet sphere.

Thus, the motivations being clear, now the question arises as to who started the war and who is responsible for it.

The strategic planning and the initial successes leave no doubt that the attack was planned and masterminded by the communists from across the border. The Communists probably thought that a system of responsible government was yet to take firm roots in South Korea, and that confusion still prevailed at the time due to factionalism among the leaders of the political parties in South Korea.

Thus, on the early Sunday morning of June 25, 1950, the North Korean forces crossed the 38th parallel and advanced to the south and claimed that they had taken action against the South Korean armed attack on the north. However, a study of the broadcast of Radio Pyongyang and other documents, leaves no doubt that the attack came from North Korea in order to unify the two halves by use of armed forces. After three days of their initial attack, the North Korean forces captured Seoul and announced that the 'final victory of the people' had been achieved and that the North Korean forces would overthrow the 'traitorous Syngman Rhee gang'. After the capture of Seoul, they also declared that the 38th parallel did not exist any longer as a demarcation line. However, the South Koreans immediately informed the United Nations Commission about the North Korean attack, and requested the United States for necessary help. The United States decided to intervene in South Korea against the northern communist attack, in defence of democratic values and to contain communist expansionism. It has also been interpreted that the United States decided to intervene in South Korea in order to contain Stalin's campaign for the conquest of the world. Stalin's policy of world communist conquest created a furore throughout the world among the free democracies and many raised their voices in the United Nations, against the communist expansionism and particularly against the aggression on South Korea. Stalin died in 1953 but the mass campaign against his policies, including the Korean war decision, in the Kremlin Camps, itself testifies to the nature of the judgement and stands in evidence in the history of the International Communist Movement that the policy of armed occupation of the border land democracies has not been a just and logical policy. It is relevant to mention here that the Soviet armed intervention in Afghanistan may hardly be considered as a wise and just policy by the successive generation of leadership in view of the fact that Afghanistan may continue to remain an ulcer within the womb of the International Communist Movement. The country of Afghanistan is inherited by the kind of tribal people, who have never accepted throughout history, the domination of Kabul, although they have not refuted the legitimacy of the government in Kabul for the last 200 to 300 years.

Stalin's decision to launch war on South Korea, among other actors, also cost him unpopularity in his own country after his death. However, once the communist aggression had started, it became a liability of the Communist International and Mao Tse-tung, who had just established a communist government in China with Soviet help. They became morally bound to extend massive armed and logistic support to North Korea as a token of his loyalty to Kremlin and to the Communist International on the whole. Thus, the massive Soviet support, particularly the decision of Stalin, which was responsible for initiating the attack was soon replaced by the Chinese in the war operational zone. The decline of the number of Soviet armed forces, as compared to the Chinese forces, also indicated that within the Kremlin Politbureau there were doubts on the utility of the war. The war, which lasted for 3 years, was mostly supported by the Chinese forces, since it was convenient for them to send reinforcements from Kirin, Shenyang and Liaoning provinces in view of the geographical proximity.

The U.N. Security Council adopted a resolution on June 25, holding the North Korean regime responsible for the aggression and called for the immediate cessation of the hostilities. The resolution also asked for the immediate withdrawal of the North Korean armed forces to the 38th parallel and called upon all the members to render every possible assistance to the United Nations in the implementation of this resolution. Similarly, President Truman ordered the United States Army, Navy and Air Units to extend all possible support to the government of the Republic of Korea. He designated General Mac Arthur as the Commanding General of the Unified Command for the United Nations forces. General Mac Arthur on the request of the South Korean government incorporated the South Korean armed forces also into the United Nations Unified Command.

The initial confrontation between the Unified Command and the communist forces resulted in the communist capture of Taejon. which enhanced the morale of the communist forces, but the continued bombing of North Korea by the naval forces of the Unified Command, continued to develop a suspense in the North Korean leadership regarding the ultimate success of their initiative. Although the North Korean press and publicity media continued to term the Korean War as a civil war, yet it had little impact on the South Korean people. On the contrary, it made them more conscious of the defence of democratic values of South Korea against the northern communist approach. Thus, President Syngman Rhee urged the South Koreans to unite and resist the communist aggression and even to unify Korea under the leadership of the Government of the Republic of Korea.

However, with the increased operational exercises of the Unified Command, the shift in the balance of power began to manifest in favour of the Republic of Korea. The discussions in the United Nations, as a result of the renewed participation of the Soviet delegate in the Security Council also called upon the North Korean troops to withdraw to the 38th parallel, from where they had started their aggression. India took an active part in the United Nations discussions and the Indian delegate proposed that a committee of non-permanent council members should be appointed to consider the Korean problem after the withdrawal of the North Korean forces. The Soviet Foreign Minister Andrei Vyshinsky introduced a resolution in the United Nations, which called for:

(1)  an immediate ceasefire in Korea;
(2)  withdrawal of all foreign troops;
(3)  an all-Korean election under the observation of a United Nations Commission;
(4)  a Joint North-South Korean Commission with equal representation of both the sides;
(5)  economic assistance to Korea;
(6)  admission of a re-constituted Korean government to the United Nations.

However, this resolution was defeated in the United Nations General Assembly which approved the earlier proposal put forward by 8 nations stipulating the creation of the United Nations Commission for the unification and rehabilitation of Korea.

With the compulsions of International Communist Movement, under Chinese leadership, and the intervention of the Chinese Peoples 'volunteers', the Korean War escalated and a new chapter was opened in the operational exercises. These communist forces were 'highly trained and indoctrinated'.[14]

The Chinese armed intervention in the Korean conflict, however, raised a furore in the United Nations, and on November 10, 1950, a draft resolution called upon China to withdraw its forces from Korea. The Chinese forces, however, with total disregard to the United Nations, continued their military exercises in Korea. Also the possibility of a ceasefire in Korea was discussed in accordance with the Charter of United Nations, in which the Arabs and other Asian nations took an active part.

On the other hand in North Korea, the attack on the South was called by Kim Il Sung as the 'national liberation struggle against the American imperialists' in his reports to the Central Standing Committee of the Democratic Front on November 19, 1950. Subsequently, in a meeting of the Central Committee of the Korean Workers Party held on December 4, 1950, Kim Il Sung reported that in the first two stages of the war, the North Korean army had over-run most of the South Korean territory, but was forced to retreat due to foreign intervention. He held that the aim of the North Korean and Chinese forces at that stage was national unification by expelling the American imperialists from the Korean soil.[15]

However, talk of ceasefire began and there were indications of change in Kremlin's attitude when Moscow demanded a new conference of all the countries, concerned with Korean cause at the World Peace Council meeting held in East Berlin on February 25, 1951. Another indication on the part of Kremlin in favour of a ceasefire was the unusual publicity given by the Soviet press and publicity media to a resolution of the United States Senator Edwin C. Johnson calling for 'an immediate ceasefire and armistice alongwith the 38th parallel'. Subsequently, the American and Canadian delegates to the United Nations also asked for an immediate ceasefire and maintaining a status quo at the 38th parallel. The Soviet representative to the United Nations Mr. Jacob Malik also emphasised the necessity of a ceasefire and armistice providing for the mutual withdrawal of armed forces from the 38th parallel. China immediately supported the Soviet proposal. Thus, it was held that the United Nations Commanders posted at the 38th parallel may conduct such military negotiations as desired by the United States and the U.S.S.R. and may leave the political questions for future discussions. Therefore, an agreement was finally reached on July 8, 1951 providing for a meeting in Kaesong city, between the representatives of the United Nations command on the one hand and Chinese and North Korean communists on the other, in order to conduct preliminary negotiations.

Professor Hak Joon Kim examines the reactions of the South and North Korean governments in the following words: 'The reaction of the ROK to the ceasefire negotiations was at the outset completely negative'. On May 28, President Rhee had already declared that: 'Nothing will make us retreat by one single step or agree to any compromise until we have driven the enemy out of Korea and achieved the unification of the country'. After Malik's proposal, Rhee repeated that theme and made it clear that unification of Korea was the minimum requirement of the Republic of Korea.[16] However, when the prospect for a truce became clear, South Korea indicated its willingness for compromise. South Korea proposed a five-point program for a ceasefire agreement. The five points were:

(1) The Chinese Communist troops will withdraw completely to Manchuria;

(2) the North Korean troops will be disarmed;

(3) the United Nations will agree to prevent third powers from aiding the North Korean Communist Party militarily, financially or by other means;

(4) the official delegates of the South Korea will participate in any international conference or meeting to discuss or consider the Korean question wholly or partially; and

(5) any proposal or action violating the sovereignty or territory of the South Korea will have no legal effect.[17]

In content, however, the above five-point program was tantamount to opposition to a ceasefire in the light of its unacceptability to the Communist side as well as to the United Nations also.[18] On the other hand, the program evidenced South Korea's concern for its security from perceived threats of aggression by communist forces after the armistice. On July 10, 1951, the opening day of truce talks, the South Korean Government advanced another program. It envisaged free elections in North Korea alone and rejected a south-north Korean coalition government.[19] This and the five-point program represented the position of South Korea on ceasefire up to July 1953, when the actual armistice agreement was signed. This posture was accompanied by constant campaigns of opposition to the truce talks.

The North Korean regime seemed, at first, to have been reluctant to accept ceasefire talks proposed by the Soviet Union. For three days, the North Korean papers and broadcasts kept silent on the Malik speech. It was not until June 26 that the North Korean official broadcast made its first mention of the Malik proposal without comment.[20] As noted earlier, the North Korean leaders may have interpreted a ceasefire as international pressure on them to abandon their idea of unification by force, whose prospect seemed to them not so dark. However, the modification of the North Korean position was clearly evidenced on the following day. An official Pyongyang radio broadcast changed its slogan of 'drive the enemy from Korean soil' to 'drive the enemy to the 38th parallel'.[21] On July 1, Kim Il Sung formally agreed to the ceasefire proposal. 'As a result of the failure of the American military adventure in Korea and because of world opinion', he claimed, the United States was 'forced to propose a ceasefire.' Since Pyongyang had 'long advocated the peaceful solution of the Korean question, it accepted the proposal', he stressed.[22]

Now the question arises what was the main concern of North Korea as regards the truce talks? According to the North Korean official statements, it was the withdrawal of foreign troops from Korea which 'would form the condition for the solution of the Korean question by the Koreans themselves'.[23] This has been interpreted by the South Koreans as 'North Korean camouflage' for their ambition to 'take over South Korea by military means', and was thus not acceptable to them. However, this North Korean point, with some variations, formed the core of the North Korean proposals at the truce talks.

The preliminary meetings for the truce talks opened in the city of Kaesong, on July 10, 1951, in accordance with the agreement, which was finally reached on July 9, 1951, called for a meeting of the representatives of the United Nations Command, the Chinese and the North Korea. The communist representatives proposed at the Kaesong meeting that the 38th parallel should be the military demarcation line between the South and the North and asked for the establishment of a demilitarised zone and the withdrawal of foreign armed forces from Korea. The proposals put forward by the representatives of the United Nations Command included an agreement on a demilitarised zone across Korea and the cessation of hostilities so as to ensure peace. After a long discussion, the agenda, that was agreed upon between the two parties, included constructive attempts for a ceasefire and armistice, the fixing of a demarcation line between the two opposing armed forces so as to establish a demilitarised zone, and make recommendations to the respective governments.

Thus, the truce talks opened on July 17, 1951, to discuss the items put in the above agenda in Panmunjom. The representatives of both the sides agreed to recommend to the two governments to hold a political conference within 90 days of the signing of the armistice. On the question of making concrete arrangements for achieving a ceasefire and armistice, the communists proposed 'the cessation of all hostilities from the day on which the armistice was signed and the withdrawal of all armed forces from the demilitarised zone within the next few days and the other areas on the opposite side within 5 days of the signing of an armistice.'[24] On the other hand, the United Nations Command delegation 'submitted seven general proposals relevant to these questions, two of which encountered opposition from the other side. These proposals provided that there should be no increase of military forces, supplies, equipments or facilities by either side after the armistice was signed and that the armistice commission should have freedom of movement throughout the whole of Korea'.[25]

Nevertheless an agreement was finally reached on the question of ceasefire and armistice and it was decided to stop the hostilities within 12 hours after the armistice was signed and both the sides would withdraw their forces from the demilitarised zone within 72 hours after the armistice became effective. The two sides also agreed that a Four-power Neutral Nations Supervisory Commission, consisting of Switzerland, Sweden, Czechoslovakia and Poland would supervise the implementation of the terms of the armistice. The issue of the prisoners of war was, however, difficult to settle. On this issue, the deadlock continued till May, 1953, when the United Nations Command submitted fresh proposals. The communists considered these proposals and after further discussions and changes in these proposals, in June, the two sides ultimately signed the Prisoners of War Agreement, which led to the final signing of the armistice agreement on July 27, 1953 thus ending the 3-year-long Korean War.

The armistice agreement, however, could not eliminate the deterrence prevailing among the South Koreans of the possibility of another North Korean attack and the security concept against any further communist aggression continued to prevail over all other important matters. Thus, President Syngman Rhee proposed a defence pact with the United States ensuring against any further communist attack. After the negotiations, Seoul was convinced of all possible political and economic support as well as a Mutual Defence Pact against any communist aggression. Seoul was also assured that in the event of another communist attack, the 16 United Nations states would again unite to repel the communist aggression promptly. It is significant that the Soviet willingness for an armistice came from their concern for strategic defence and fear of losing the northern half of Korea to the United Nations Forces It is believed that had the Kremlin leaders not taken the initiative to compromise, the Unified Command Forces could have run over North Korea. Also the two Super Powers had entered an era of cold war by this time and any successful attempt at the liberation of the people of North Korea from the totalitarian regime would have caused relative political and strategic repercussions in East European communist-occupied states. The Kremlin was engaged enough in consolidating her post-war gains and could not afford to lose her grip on any of these occupied states. The liberation of any of these states, whether in the Far-East or in the Near-East, could have been a fatal blow to the International Communist Movement and to Kremlin in her significant political and strategic operations.

It is interesting to add here that in any large-scale Kremlin propaganda after World War II, the communisation of North Korea, East Germany, and the Near-Eastern states was held as a great victory for workers of those countries under the banner of proletarian internationalism. It is therefore easily understandable that the post-war strategic decisions of the Allied Powers had only led the Russians to occupy these smaller countries in view of establishing 'peace'. Thus, the Marxist theory of 'Dialectical Materialism' was hardly responsible for the communisation of North Korea, East Germany and East European states; rather it was a 'forced communisation' and a forced establishment of a totalitarian state under Kremlin leadership, that was responsible for the establishment of these totalitarian regimes. This has to be recognised as a new phenomenon within the framework of the concept of 'Dialectical Materialism' that when the workers of the world failed to unite for a common cause due to varying political, social and economic conditions in different sections of international society, the middle-aged concept of forced baptisation of the people to the cause of Marxism-Leninism was ultimately exercised by Kremlin. The latest example of Soviet armed intervention in Afghanistan is probably the most suitable one in this regard to understand, analyse, assess and conclude, whether it was the workers or the majority of people of Afghanistan that rose in revolt for the cause of proletarian internationalism or was it Kremlin's policy of forced baptisation of the people of Afghanistan, in total disregard to the will and aspirations of the majority of the people of Afghanistan.

# CHAPTER IV

# SUPER POWERS AND THE KOREAN CONFLICT

## The Bipolarity in Triangulation of Relationship

The Super Power involvement within the mechanics of the Korean conflict is the most important aspect of the whole complex situation in which the Korean conflict emerged, developed and is maintaining a status-quo, pending a final peaceful resolution. The conflict has often been assessed in view of North-South Korean compulsions, nationalist aspirations and will of the people, adroitness either on the part of Kim Il Sung or the southern leaders, and the political and ideological developments on the peninsula which have an impact on the 'peaceful' approaches to national reunification.[26]

### Sino-US hard bargaining exercises :

It is significant that change in the United States foreign policy, with the beginning of the 70s, was directed towards reducing her escalated involvement in the Far-East and South-East Asia, with a motive to improve bilateral relations with China, since it let loose new strategies which were responsible for the emergence of a new balance of power system in East Asia and South-East Asia. [27] The United States decision to gradually withdraw from the Vietnamese conflict set in motion the reassessment of her policies in other countries of East Asia.

The policy of containment of communism in South-East Asia had led the policy planners to believe that the continued United States opposition to both China and the Soviet Union may identify common interests of the two communist powers in their

46

common programme of defeating the "United States Imperialists".[28] Besides, the unending military involvement of the United States on the other side of the globe, the unnecessary drain in economy, the criticism of the United States in international press and publicity and several other factors had led to a national debate oriented towards assessing the utility of the United States involvement in Vietnam. These were the two factors that led the United States to conduct a reappraisal of her policies in the Far-East and a beginning was made for the opening of a bilateral dialogue with Dr. Kissinger's visit to Peking in January 1972. Although a beginning had already been in progress, reportedly with the meeting of the delegates of the two countries at Warsaw and other places, yet the world came to know about it only in January 1972. This was followed by President Nixon's visit to Peking and President Nixon's "Guam Doctrine", which is very significant from the point of view of the United States strategic involvement in East Asia. Although the doctrine was meant to please the Chinese leaders, yet it heralded a new era of partnerships and ultimately led to the beginning of the emergence of the Japanese imperialism and increased Japanese involvement in East Asian conflicts.

President Nixon's "Guan Doctrine" and his Peking visit also caused political and strategic setbacks to Kremlin as it led to increased Chinese and Japanese involvement in East Asian and international politics, Chinese admission to the Security Council of the United Nations and an almost eclipse of Kremlin's effective involvement in East Asia. China's admission to the Security Council was also an important development since it heralded a new era of Sino-American co-operation on various regional and international complicated issues.

Under ideological compulsions and the political and strategic framework in the East Asian complex situation and in view of exercising the 'Brezhnev Doctrine' in North Korea, the Soviet Union had once opened its mind about attacking China, if the United States could tacitly approve such a plan. Hence the very existence of such a notion in Kremlin to forcibly occupy China has led political analysts and observers to believe that armed occupation of a neighbouring country has been the guiding point in Kremlin's approach to set the affairs of a neighbouring troubled socialist state in order, within the concept of the dogmatic framework of the "Brezhnev Doctrine". Haldeman's disclosure thus, determines the nature and extent of the operational mechanics of the "Brezhnev Doctrine." This concept is not only non-existent in the original scientific doctrine of "Dialectical Materialism", but even now, if a free and fair referendum is sought within the workers of the communist camps, probably armed occupation of China by the Soviet Union would not be approved.

With a view to exercising greater influence on world affairs and greater control over the dilapidated complex situation in South-East and the East Asian region vis-a-vis the Soviet Union, China made a reappraisal of her policies towards United States which were more strategic than political. An indication in this direction was given in Lin Piao's report dealing with Chinese foreign relations to the Ninth Congress of the Chinese Communist Party held in April, 1969, which had formally brought the cultural revolution to an end and had criticised the Soviet Union policies more than the United States.[29] However, the Soviet armed occupation of Czechoslovakia in August 1968 also reminded the Chinese of Soviet expansionist designs by means of armed occupation under the "Brezhnev Doctrine". It was apprehended in Peking that the Soviet Union may have an eye on the Chinese capital particularly a Soviet attack on Chinese nuclear installations seemed probable.

It is believed that Kremlin's proposal of a proposed attack on China, to the United States was suitably exploited by Dr. Henry Kissinger to win over the Chinese and to broaden the gap between China and the Soviet Union. It may also be considered a great success on the part of Dr. Henry Kissinger to be able to develop friendly relations with China by convincing Peking about Moscow's ill-designs and thereby settle the American score in Vietnam.

In view of the Sino-Soviet conflict an important factor that contributed towards the Sino-American rapproachment was the ideological clash which came to a new height during the late sixties. The massive propaganda by the Soviet Union against the Chinese in the late sixties was a compelling factor on the part of the Chinese to accept any offer from the United States for a mutual normalisation of her relations with her. Besides, the Chinese also aspired to gain a permanent membership of the Security Council of the United Nations, with the help of the United States, which was believed to be a pre-condition set by Peking for normalisation of relations.

By getting a permanent seat in the Security Council with the help of the United States, the Chinese could well carry on their effective counter-moves against the Soviet Union and re-assert their policies in the United Nations. This was, however, a major concession given by the United States to China and thus it has been accused that China gained more than the United States in the process of normalisation of their bilateral relations. The Chinese may also be grateful for the American withdrawal from Vietnam since the beginning of the normalisation process had its due impact on the United States' foreign policy in South-East Asia, which ultimately led to the complete withdrawal of the American forces. For the Americans also, the concessions given to the Chinese were a profitable bargain from the point of view of the national interests of the United States, as she was at least able to balance better her relationship with the Soviet Union after her improved ties with the Chinese. It more or less meant an encirclement of the Soviet Union with Chinese partnership and posed a major challenge to Moscow's influence in East Asia.

The Chinese exercise in hard bargaining, in defence of their national interests is also visible in their behaviour during the visits of Cyrus Vance and Dr. Brzezinski to Peking to study the Chinese mind in expanding cooperation. Any possible attempt on the part of the United States to negotiate the Taiwan issue was to be reverted back by the Chinese with repeated offensive statements coded in usual ideological terminology like 'appeasement' and 'hegemony', since the Chinese believed that they were in a comfortable position in their relations with the United States; and by gaining more and more time they would be able to strengthen their strategic position by becoming stronger economically as well as militarily.

It is significant that the delay in completing the process of normalisation was likely to be accompanied by 'erosion of support' for the normalisation policy in the United States; overtime opposition could also increase from the allies and friends, in Asia, thus making the task of normalisation and an eventual decision more problematic. Keeping in view China's long-term interests in becoming a major 'influential power' in Asia and the Third World, the United States' own adjustments to drifting relationships in the Pacific and other developing areas could be comfortable, if the United States did not stick to the Taiwan question, thus making China feel uncomfortable. The Chinese leaders could foresee certain advantages in delay since the strategy of 'wait and watch' could enable them to overlook the difficult decision on normalisation, till she had reasonably developed her economy and modernised her armed forces.

Under the above political and strategic compulsions, the

Chinese leaders continued to beep from the bamboo curtain, hardly indicating any significant change in policy towards the United States during the visit of Dr. Brzezinski. They, however, continued to emphasise their earlier stand for establishing diplomatic relations. In official statements, they softened their hard line for establishing diplomatic relations with the United States as expressed earlier in the Shanghai Communique of 1972, into three basic conditions: (i) that the United States first of all sever diplomatic relations with the Republic of China; (ii) that the United States-Republic of China Mutual Defence Treaty of 1954 be terminated; and that (iii) all United States forces and military installations be withdrawn from the Republic of China. Since 1973 the Chinese officials have continued to assert to American visitors these 'three conditions' for establishing normal relations with the United States.

However, there was a reasonable argument in the Chinese theory that for over twenty years, Taiwan had posed a direct political and strategic challenge and a positive military threat to communist China and that it also provided an 'attractive alternative' vis-a-vis a communist system and way of life. The Chinese view was understandable that as long as Taiwan claimed sovereignty over all of China, followed anti-communist policies, and conducted both 'open propaganda' and 'clandestine activities' against mainland China, it would continue to constitute a potential threat to the mainland.

Dr. Brzezinski, like Cyrus Vance, however, cautiously and diplomatically avoided any sharp comment that might convey an impression that the Chinese opposition to continued United States ties with Taiwan, had softened. He diplomatically set aside any deliberation on the Taiwan question and rather concentrated on the important strategic question of how to co-operate with Peking in frustrating Soviet designs in the underdeveloped and the developing world. The attitude of Dr. Brzezinski indicated a clear warning to Kremlin in her global designs and a counterforce in establishing peace in the world. Dr. Brzezinski asserted both at the opening and closing banquet speeches in Peking: "Only those aspiring to dominate others have any reason to fear the further development of American-Chinese relations."

Dr. Brzezinski's diplomatic approach in expressing in public his 'suspicions' about Moscow understandably pleased the Chinese who had received a comparatively softer line from Vance earlier. Dr. Brzezinski warned the Soviet Union against "global or regional hegemony" and humorously called USSR a "polar bear", during his visit to the Great Wall. Significantly, the Chinese expressions during Dr. Brzezinski's trip to China, had also been mild compared to those during the visit of Cyrus Vance in August, since they were almost pleased with Dr. Brzezinski's tougher anti-Soviet remarks. This is significant because during Cyrus Vance's visit to Peking, Vice-Premier Teng Hsiao-ping had sharply reacted in an interview with the American visitors in September, by calling the Vance trip a "step backward." Thus, the anti-Kremlin hardliner, Dr. Brzezinski's Peking visit was diplomatic success.

On the question of the United States policy of selling arms to China, it is noteworthy that the Chinese interests in buying Western technology considerably increased after the death of Mao and the West's positive response also grew simultaneously. Britain had expressed her willingness to supply the Harrier vertical take-off aircraft, and had reportedly sold the Spey aircraft engine for Chinese fighters. The United States, under these circumstances, had no option but to appease the Chinese by expanding more bilateral trade on Chinese terms as well as to support the Chinese diplomatically in the extension of her influence over Asian and the developing countries.

It has rightly been suggested by western analysts that Dr. Brzezinski, more than most officials in the administration, had been particularly interested in trying to exploit the Sino-Soviet split to the disadvantage of the Russians. Thus he had been keen to find some common political ground with the Chinese and understandably supported certain NATO countries for sale of arms to the Chinese. The United States administration had decided against providing China with any American military equipment, yet some officials were believed to be inclined to favour the sale of certain defensive weapon systems to China through West-European countries. In interviews with administration officials on the eve of Dr. Brzezinski's trip to China there had been indications that if France and Britain sought permission, within the alliance, to sell defensive equipment to China, the United States may probably welcome the decision. France had accordingly held discussions with China on the sale of an anti-tank missile, known as HOT. Britain, which had earlier sold China Rolls Royce Spey jet engines for use in fighter planes, has been discussing the sale of the Harrier vertical-takeoff plane.

However, there was an important implication in such an exercise that before such sales could be completed, they had to be approved by NATO's special co-ordinating committee due to the advice of the member countries against selling military equipment or military related technology to communist countries. However, exceptions may be made, and member countries were not necessarily bound by the committee's rulings. According to western analysts, a senior United States administration official had once indicated that although the White House had earlier decided that the United States would not sell military equipment to China it had no firm policy on whether to approve or object to sales by Western allies.

The Sino-American rapprochement had a definite impact on the Korean unification question and an important break in the deadlock could be assessed with the compulsions on the North Korean leaders for agreeing to sit with the South Korean leaders on August 20, 1971 in Panmunjom to discuss non-political humanitarian questions. The discussions that followed for several months ultimately resulted in the issue of a Joint Communique signed by the representatives of the South and North, on July 4, 1972, in which they agreed on the three principles for national unification : (1) Unification to be achieved through independent Korean efforts without being subjected to foreign pressure and interference; (2) Unification to be achieved through peaceful means and not by the use of force against each other; and (3) an expression of sincere desire for national unity irrespective of the ideas and ideologies. The communique also emphasised the easing of tensions between the South and North; to carry out exchanges in many fields and to make an early success in the ongoing Red Cross Talks. This meeting between the South and North at Panmunjom and the issue of the Joint Communique has probably been the only important constructive landmark, in which North Korea also participated and expressed her willingness on certain fundamental points as indicated in the Joint Communique and was an important step towards the process of unification, under the compulsions of the changing political and strategic situation in East Asia.

### Impact on Korean conflict

However, the most important question, in regard to an objective study of the Korean conflict, is the respective attitudes, **the** inbuilt political, ideological and strategic interests and intensive involvement of the Super Powers within the mechanics of the Korean conflict in the broad framework of North-East and East Asian political and strategic complex situation.

As discussed in the earlier chapters, the two Super Powers share full responsibility for the beginning of the Korean conflict, as is evident from the nature and extent of the conflict.

In the process of looting the Japanese booty, the fact that the Soviet Union was a major communist power was well known, the compulsions of the Marxist 'Dialectical Materialism' were well understood, the 'imperial' content within the framework for 'Dialectical Materialism' could have been well assessed and visualised and Kremlin had already scored major gains in Eastern Europe as a 'prize' for her involvement against the Nazis and Hitler. But probably half a decade long bitter involvement of the Allied Forces against Germany and Japan compelled the heads of states to concentrate more on the strategic situations and reparations in the hours of triumph, and could hardly visualise the built-in political implications within their strategic but hasty decision.

The conflict in the Korean peninsula represents the Super Powers' recalcitrant attitude toward a just settlement of the post-World War II problems, and which may be accounted for more by a lack of political analysis as well as a total disregard for academic assessment of political and strategic aspects of the conflicts in perspective. I think this is why we find, in post-World War II decades, a revolutionary spurt in academic analyses within and much more outside governments, in assessing and visualising the implications and overall impact in the respective behavioural approaches, in view of their own interests in the dynamic conflict culture.

As the Korean peninsula represents a small emblem of conflict between totalitarianism v/s free democracy, the most unfortunate contribution of the Second World War has been the division of international forces into two opposing groups—each struggling for its existence against the other. The smaller regional or bilateral offshoots, whether nationalist or independent, are the products of the major conflict between the two Super Powers representing two opposing forces and living in a state of struggle for existence.

In the complexity of the conflict the intensity of the major one has the capacity to absorb the minor one, but each minor one has the potential to emerge as a major one.[30]

Whether in the context of the Korean conflict or **any other** regional or bilateral conflicts between the two Super Powers, it is to be understood in the above context. The behavioural dynamics and the conditioning process of the two Super Powers are governed under regulated mechanics of superiority in their bitter involvement in the struggle for existence.

In the Korean context, North Korea's foreign policy and internal major political developments, having certain political impact on foreign policy, have to be understood in the bipolarity of its relationship with the Soviet Union and China within the framework of the International Communist Movement. It is much more significant in the case of North Korea since it may become the scapegoat of the exercise of mutual power-struggle in the ultimate course of the trial of strength between the Soviet Union and China in the efflorescence of their conflict. As discussed earlier, Kim Il Sung has successfully balanced his personal and state security by playing between the two, and neither of them could afford to offend him under deterrence that he may totally align himself with the other.

### Soviet Union and North Korea

From the Soviet Union and Chinese points of view, North Korea is not only of political significance but much more of strategic relevance, since to the Soviet Union it offers, among other things, a non-freezing sea port in furtherance of its strategic interests, in the sea of Japan, in liaison with its overall strategic exercises in the North-West Pacific; and to China it offers a major political base to counter Soviet expansionist designs in the region, since China claims its historical dominance over the region.

this context, it is significant to remember an open secret, known to concerned strategists that the Soviet Union has been able to gain total concessions from North Korea to exercise an exclusive control over NAJIN non-freezing sea port of North Korea, in close strategic liaison with Vladivostok for its own advantage in the Sea of Japan. North Korea has five international sea ports for trade and naval operations, excluding the NAJIN seaport, which probably falls under one of the classified navigation ports, exclusively reserved for the Russians. Notably, North Korea does not include NAJIN seaport in its list of international seaports. As the reports indicate, the port was developed by the Russians probably in mid-seventies, for trade navigation facilities for the transport of its Siberian goods overseas. Even Kremlin has once admitted, quoting a statement of Mrs. Varunamova, a liaison officer of the Ministry of Transport of the Soviet Union, that the railroad employees of the Soviet Union transport coal, chemical products, lumber and fertilizer to Dumangang railroad station, which is located near the Russian and North Korean border line for onward shipment.[31] It is said that at Dumangang railroad station the goods are handed over to the North Koreans for loading at the NAJIN seaport for overseas transport.[32] Although NAJIN seaport is reported to be operated by the North Koreans, the possibility of Russian presence cannot be totally ruled out.

However, the failure on the part of North Koreans to include NAJIN seaport in the list of their international seaports, is evidence that the port enjoys exclusive or 'sovereign' 'right of use' by the Russians for their overseas operations.

The above single example is very significant, among several others, and indicates the nature and extent of involvement of the Soviet Union, of late, strategically and the accommodation and friendliness that North Korea has exhibited towards the Soviet Union. It is to be remembered that the Soviet Union has well-known political and strategic stakes in the North-West Pacific and has reason to act in defence of those stakes.

It is significant to understand, in the Korean context, that the geographical priorities of Soviet global strategy have a behavioral 'relationship both to the security needs of the Soviet Union and to the demands of the global power-game.'[33] The Soviet strategic security of its home territory, including its strategic borderland along the North-West Pacific, is of prime importance to the Soviet Union, in view of the Sino-Soviet conflict and particularly in view of the US strategic presence, and the developing conflict between the two rivals threatens even an armed confrontation, going to the extent of even a possible strategic nuclear war. The East-Asian theatre complex, including the Korean peninsula, is of similar strategic concern in terms of Soviet territorial security. This may be understood in view of the enhanced Soviet concern for East Asia, which is evident in its effort, for defensive and economic reasons, to decentralise its lopsided concentration in the European part of the Soviet Union and disperse into territory, East of the Urals.[34]

Professor Robert A. Scalapino has examined the Soviet treatment of North Korea in two seperate themes. The first is that the

Soviet 'assistance to the North Korean policy has been extensive, continuous and of major importance since the initial post-war years'.[35] Similar to that of the Chinese, what is equally cognizant of its assistance provided to Kim Il Sung in establishing a communist regime, in north of the peninsula, and expresses boldly in terms of North Korean people's gratitude to the Soviet Union for the cause. A Soviet military journalists delegation, which visited North Korea in mid-1970 reported after their return from North Korea, that there exists a 'profound gratitude' in the Korean people for Soviet Union's 'constant support' to North Korea, which reminds us of the spirit of August days of 1945 when Soviet soldiers had landed in Korea for the cause of "fulfilling their international duty".[36] Soviet support, it is said, is still alive in 'multiplying the strengthening of friendship between the Soviet and Korean peoples, and the growing cooperation between the two countries', it is asserted, continues to be 'based upon loyalty to Marxism-Leninism and proletarian internationalism'.[37] Another Soviet recent report stresses that the Korean people in their hour of need "were not alone".[38] Reminding Kim Il Sung of the massive Soviet support during the Korean War, the author, without mentioning the Chinese support, quotes Kim as saying: 'at a very difficult time for our motherland, the Soviet Union, as the head of the democratic forces of the whole world, gave the Korean people massive aid and support'.[39]

The second theme, according to Professor Robert A. Scalapino, that is in fashion among Soviet spokesmen, is to feature the 'brilliant successes' of North Korea since its emergence, again with considerable emphasis upon the contributions of the Soviet Union to those successes.[40] Significantly, constant reminders are being served to the North Korean people that these 'brilliant achievements' are due to the 'friendship and unity between the Soviet Union and the DPRK, born in the flames of endless struggle and developed and strengthened on the joint road taught by the great Lenin'.[41] Besides, the Soviet Union is also credited for having provided massive economic and technical assistance for building up enterprises which account for about 60% of electricity, 45% of iron ore, 34% of rolled metal, 30% of steel and 20% of textiles.[42]

Although these exercises in 'Soviet self-congratulations and even the encomiums heaped upon North Korea' are not new, it is significant that these exercises mean to serve as constant reminders to North Korea to maintain a continued loyal attitude toward the

Soviet Union in response to the latter's support extended in the 'hour of need'. This seems to be a sophisticated warning from the Soviet Union to the leadership in North Korea against such developments like 'Juche' or any balancing shifts towards China.

Besides, Soviet Union also asserts complete support for Kim Il Sung's unification proposals in more explicit language and emphatic words. The Soviet Union asserts Kim Il Sung's three principles and five points on unification as realistic proposals, reflecting the will of the entire people and that the responsibility of the current impasse 'lies with the Seoul regime and US imperialism'.[43] Pravda and Izvestia, the leading organs of the Soviet Communist Party and state, continue to launch scathing attacks on South Korea and the 'US imperialists', with a stronger voice and tougher support for Kim Il Sung than those in 1970s. The Soviet press and publicity media also club the Chinese with 'US imperialists,' while reassuring the Koreans that "the patriotic aspirations of the Koreans are dear and comprehensible to the Soviet Union, and has always supported them and will support them in the future".[44]

The above few references evidence the general current attitude of the Soviet Union, which speaks of emphatic support for North Korea. As discussed earlier, while it speaks of the desired constant loyalty of North Korea towards Soviet Union, it is also possible that North Korea may exploit the Soviet's repeated emphasis in gaining more and more economic aid and armed assistance reminding the Kremlin authorities to 'translate promising words into bountiful action'.[45]

It is a fact to be remembered that Kim Il Sung himself could not have achieved leadership except for Soviet support. In the early years North Korean leadership accepted total Soviet guidance on every issue, which was evident from the unswerving allegiance to Stalin, on his death, in official organ's panegyrics as 'our beloved father and leader'. The continuance of a single leadership from 1945 onwards is enough to feel allegiance and loyalty to the Soviet Union, besides political and strategic considerations.

However, with the beginning of the conflict, between Moscow and Peking, during the middle of the fifties, we find the beginning of an independent North Korean attitude towards the Soviet Union; and from the mid-sixties, i.e. from the Cultural Revolution, a major shift is discernible from the critical assessment of the Soviet policies in somewhat Chinese expressions. But simultaneously a constant, though casual in nature, tribute continued to be paid to the Soviets for their assistance, both strategic and economic, for the reconstruction of North Korea.

Apart from this, in the North Korean-Soviet Union relations, we find a great lull in the second half of the seventies in view of the fact that since 1975, the Soviet Union has reportedly refused to receive Kim Il Sung. In January, 1977, Pak Song Chul, Prime Minister of North Korea, had visited Moscow in order to collect more economic aid but reportedly his request was flatly refused. North Korea had also adopted a critical view of Vietnamese invasion on Cambodia and Hanoi's involvement, while remaining silent on the subsequent Chinese incursions into Vietnam. Besides, Sihanouk has been a frequent guest of Kim Il Sung and accorded a royal treatment in Pyongyang, although he has been an anathema both to the Russians and Vietnamese. As late as August 1980, North Korean Vice-Premier Kim Kyong Yon, during his visit to Kuala Lumpur, stressed that North Korea supported the ASEAN demand for the withdrawal of Vietnamese troops from Cambodia.

Significantly, a somewhat contradictory trend is also visible in North Korean attitude on certain other issues as well. For example, on the 20th anniversary of the establishment of North Korean-Cuban relations, "Nodong Sinmun" praised the Vietnamese people and expressed the hope that friendly relations between 'our two peoples' would continue to develop favourably.[46]

However, North Korea's attitude on Soviet intervention in Afghanistan has been to praise the 'victory' of the 'revolution' as 'an event of great significance in the struggle of the Afghan people for consolidating national independence and achieving the independent development of the country', significantly without any reference to the Soviet Union, which makes it seem as if the Soviet Union had no role to play, in spite of the fact that the 'revolution' and the reported 'success' involved about 80,000 Soviet armed personnel with constant live-link support form north of the Afghan border.[47]

The above orientations in the North Korean foreign policy overtures towards the Soviet Union, are only indicative of a balance that North Korea has been trying hard to establish, but at the same time ensuring that these exercises may not be at the cost of Kim's 'cemented-in-blood' friendship with the Chinese.

## China and North Korea

In view of the above, while examining Chinese friendly overtures and the recent attitude and policies towards North Korea, we find that the Chinese expressions of sympathy and cooperation have been more sentimental and colourful like Vice-Premier Che Peng Fi's pronouncement in mid-1970 of a 'militant friendship' which has been 'cemented in blood'. China consistently maintains a firm commitment to the security of North Korea and strongly defends North Korea's 'one Korea' approach, in spite of her somewhat flexible attitude towards South Korea. There has hardly been an evidence in support of a basic change in Chinese stand on North Korean unification formula even after Chinese normalisation of relations with the United States. Deng Xiaoping's statements in Peking, Washington and Tokyo attest to the Chinese firm stand that the US should withdraw her troops from South Korea to facilitate the unification of Korea and that the US government should enter into direct negotiations with North Korea for the resolution of the Korean conflict.

Chinese close relations with North Korea have been continuously strengthened by frequent exchanges of military and economic delegations between the two countries. In spite of its weak economic posture, China has been extending continued economic assistance to North Korea. Locked in a competition with the Soviet Union, China has been selling oil to North Korea at a cheaper price and in 1976 an oil pipe line linking China with North Korea was completed. In fact, in comparison to the Soviet Union, the Chinese have sometimes delivered more armed assistance to North Korea.

We find a discernible shift in the Chinese-North Korean relations following the visit of Kim Il Sung to Peking in 1975, after a long gap since 1961. Since Kim's visit coincided with the South Vietnamese debacle, it was highly speculated that Kim Il Sung may seek Chinese support for his unification plan with the use of armed forces. Although Kim Il Sung pledged his support to a revolution in South Korea, it is believed that the Chinese pressure had been against war in the Korean peninsula. The 'Chinese were afraid of renewed hostilities on the Korean peninsula, which may destroy an emerging Sino-American detente and could lead Japan to nuclear rearmament, and may also result in greater Soviet influence on North Korea due to Pyongyang's dependence upon Soviet military aid'. However, the visits of CCP Chairman and Premier Hua Guofeng, in May 1978, and Vice Premier Deng Xiaoping in September 1978 to North Korea were believed to have further 'cemented' the mutual relationship, although no communique was issued in either of the two visits, which may indicate differences on political and strategic issues in view of Kim Il Sung's 'Juche' or independent line on Sino-Soviet conflict and emphasis on military means. Deng, in his press conference in Peking and Tokyo, said that he did not consider serious tension existed on the Korean peninsula. Deng's assessment of the strategic situation on the Korean peninsula speaks of the Chinese attitude as well as differences with the North Korean stand, which leads us to believe that China probably views a unified strong Korea to be against its political and strategic interests particularly in view of Kim's 'Juche' or independent line and the Sino-Soviet conflict.

Notwithstanding, China also maintains a strong position on opening the tripartite international conference as an attempt in the process of reunification of North and South Korea, which is indicative of Chinese acceptance and recognition of South Korea as an important party to the Korean reunification talks. Chinese Vice-Premier Deng, while talking to Japanese Kyodo News Service President Watanabe, in Peking in February 1979, said that it was necessary for both North and South Korea to hold talks on the Korean issue and significantly insisted that the US should be a party to the inter-Korean talks. It was also made clear by the Chinese that China would not be a party to an international conference on the Korean reunification issue. This was reported by Chinese leaders to UN Secretary General Kurt Waldheim, Japanese Prime Minister Ohira and to the visiting US Senators. According to US Senator, John Glenn, Vice Premier Deng said that "China has no direct responsibility in Korea". Even Kurt Waldheim admitted, after meeting Deng and Hua, that China recognised United States' important role in the Korean reunification talks without Chinese involvement as a negotiating party.

In view of the above, the balance, evident in the Chinese attitude towards the unification question, exemplifies the Chinese stand, which is different from that held by North Korea. North Korea emphasises that as far as the question of unification is concerned, there are separate problems to be solved between Pyongyang and Washington and between Pyongyang and Seoul. North Korea rejects (or offers only observer status) South Korea's inclusion in Pyongyang-Washington talks and considers any US involvement between Pyongyang-Seoul talks, as interference in the internal affairs of Korea.

It is relevant to discuss here the hypothesis of the possibility of a war on the Korean peninsula in view of the interests of the two Super Powers in the North-East Asian region. On this question, brilliant analyses have been put forward from time to time by several eminent scholars like Professors Richard L. Walker, Rudolf J. Rummel, Robert A. Scalapino, Vernon Aspaturian and several others.

The political and military balance between North and South Korea is a relevant aspect which must be taken into account in considering the possibility of a new war on the peninsula; more relevant is the balance in North-East Asia among Japan, China, the US and the Soviet Union, in light of the Sino-Soviet conflict, the security interests of the US and Japan in Korea, North Korea's relationship with and dependence on the Soviet Union and China, the tacit implications of the Sino-US and Sino-Japanese Alliances and the conflicting interests of the United States and the Soviet Union.

In the developing international political situation, the gradual stronger emphasis on war and the expanding area and periscope of the two Super powers' direct involvement evidences much bolder expressions in terms of theoretical and behavioral approaches like 'Brezhnev Doctrine'. This is significant in view of the fact that the Soviet Union is gradually surpassing the United States in conventional military power as well as strategic weapons. The Soviet will and determination to gradually enlarge her influence—beginning with East Germany, North Korea and North Vietnam, then expanding to Laos, Cambodia, the Middle-East, Cuba, El Salvador, Chile, Angola and Ethiopia and most significantly in Afghanistan—poses the possibility, although a remote possibility, of the danger of a direct confrontation with the United States in the 1980s and 1990s. In response, President Ronald Reagan and Defence Secretary Casper Weinberger's recent bold assertions to put the United States on an effective strategic foothold are very significant in this direction.

According to Soviet perceptions, in the words of Professor Rudolf J. Rummel "evidence suggests that in their stratgic calculus, giving a conservative estimate from their point of view of their weapons' capabilities and the costs of a nuclear war, they will soon, if not now, see the gains of nuclear war as outweighing its costs. More specifically, evidence shows an increasing likelihood that the Soviets could survive a nuclear war with a level of damage. If blocked by a resurgent American containment policy, the Soviets may decide to take 'advantage' of their massive military power before a 'resurgent American capability and will' again frustrate Soviet global revolutionary interests".

In weighing the possibility of another World War, in view of the ever increasing totalitarian pressure, it may be believed that a sufficient Soviet will-to-war and confidence in winning that war are more or less lacking yet the trends are evidencing both, and hence the possibility of war, although a remote possibility, cannot be totally ruled out. In the Korean context, the possibility of such an unfortunate event and the eventual outcome will have its direct repercussions.

Besides, the Soviet conventional military and strategic superiority, as seen from published evidence, particularly in view of its geographical proximity to Asia and Europe, is an important factor in determining the regional and bilateral status-quo in any given situation, e.g. Afghanistan, will be posing problematic exercises. But in the Korean context it has relative significance in terms of motivating and stimulating and thus strengthening totalitarian hard-line in Northern attitude towards 'peaceful' unification. In the Korean context, I think, this is a very significant part of the whole game which has its strong repercurative impact on the problem of unification in peace-time diplomacy.

In regard to the Soviet perception of a global war, I think Soviet deterrence of China is important, since in the hypothesis of a Super Power confrontation and Soviet Union losing, Soviet losses in Asia may be tremendous, with China tacitly occupying the Siberian lands, 'outer Mongolia' etc. In the event of an open war between the two Super Powers, the Chinese may have to decide their national interests, since the Chinese hypothesis is that in such an event they will come out as a major gainer.

Considering Soviet Union's bitter entaglement in Eastern Europe and proxy involvement in the Middle East, in defence of its foreign policy interests in a see-saw game vis-a-vis the United States, Soviet stakes are more important, since the developments, particularly in the Middle East, are in an explosive stage as compared to the Korean peninsula and an inadvertent mistake may only flutter the Hot Line. U.S. efforts for defence in the Indian Ocean and Persian Gulf and the recent US operation 'Bright Star' in Egypt is an indication in the direction.

However, any beginning of hostilities at the 38th Parallel will bring about a direct confrontation between the two Super Powers, which neither of them would like to risk in view of known consequences. In view of this I think various think-tanks have yet to explore the possibility of the Super Power conflict beginning with the Korean peninsula and thus a status-quo, and a struggle for existence may continue, pending pragmatic and final approaches, acceptable to both the North and South in the solemn cause of unification.

# CHAPTER V

# THE SEARCH FOR UNIFICATION—I

The issue not only of 'unification' but peaceful unification of the two halves of the country is the most important problem in the Korean conflict. The issue, which is basically a bilateral one in character, involves, however, certain basic interests particularly of the International Communist Movement, which do not fit in accordance with the will and aspirations of the majority of the Korean people. It is a problem between the diplomatic and strategic mechanics of totalitarian expansionism on the one hand and the defence of freedom and democracy, human rights and improved economy on the other.

The attempts for unification date back to the division of the country at the 38th parallel, when the nationalist leaders had raised their voice against any bifurcation of the country, but certain compulsions and strategic priorities, on the part of the Super Powers, on the eve of the Second World War, brought about the division at the 38th parallel. There have been numerous armed provocations, guerilla attempts of subversion and massive revolutionary propaganda from the North in an attempt at unification, which have no de facto or de jure acceptance within the framework of international law. Although there has been a strong sense of 'shared nationhood' among the people of South and North, yet the ideological compulsions have caused a continued deadlock in the peaceful unification of the country.

After the formal division of the country in 1948, there have been serious attempts for unification both from the North as well as from the South. According to Professor Hak-Joon Kim, 'the perpetuation of the division of Korea in 1948 had different meanings to the leadership of the Republic of Korea in the South and Democratic People Republic of Korea in the North. To the South Koreans, it was what they had to accept as a second choice after the spring of 1947, although they had no desire to maintain it . . . .Syngman Rhee and his followers advocated the establishment of a separate government in the South. For they believed that without so doing, South Korea would have been overthrown by well trained North Korean troops under the aegis of the Soviet forces. What most concerned them was the fear of communisation of the whole Korean peninsula. Thus their attitude was that they would rather live divided temporarily than unified under communism'.[48]

Accordingly, it is rightly believed that South and North Korea took essentially 'irreconcilable" approaches to the unification of Korea.[49] The North has persistently insisted upon the withdrawal of foreign troops and non-interference of foreign powers, including the United Nations, in the Korean conflict. According to the Southern opinion this was like a Trojan War for communisation of South Korea, but was couched in the most appealing terms of national self-determination of the Korean problem.[50] South Korea however, consistently linked the unification problem basically with the question of the security of the South against communism and has put forward an aggressive posture against the communisation problem.

On the question of legitimacy, the government of Republic of Korea held the opinion that it was the only lawful and legitimate government on the Korean peninsula since it had come into existence as a result of UN intervention, and as such the Constitution of the ROK was considered to have jurisdiction over the entire Korean peninsula and the adjacent islands.

However, the basic problem with the ROK was to gain as much international recognition as possible as being the 'only lawful government' on the peninsula. The Allies of the ROK, particularly the United States, also supported this move and at the United Nations in December 1948 the United States introduced a draft resolution urging that the United Nations accept the legitimacy of the ROK government as the 'only lawful government' on the peninsula. The communist bloc, particularly the Soviet Union questioned this proposal and submitted another one asking for the re-establishment of an independent democratic state in the peninsula.

The resolution, which was initially adopted in the General Assembly significantly declared that a lawful government had been established having effective control and jurisdiction over the part of Korea, where the temporary commission was able to observe and consult and in which the great majority of the people of all-Korea reside. The resolution also held that this government was based on election, which was a valid expression of the free will of the electorate of that part of Korea. This resolution was accepted by the ROK with the claim that the ROK is the only legal and national government in Korea.[51]

This resolution of the United Nations is significant in that it accepted the 'legality of the ROK' and it inadvertently meant that South Korean Government would recover the territory occupied by the 'illegal' communist North. This was the reason and the beginning of the southern demand for 'March North'. This was the slogan which Syngman Rhee continued to reiterate with a view to regain the northern territory. Thus the attitude of the United Nations had a basic impact on the direction of unification and resulted in a stronger demand for peaceful unification of the South and North under the leadership of the 'legally accepted regime' of the South.

The southern approach to the problem also necessitated increased armed forces and tightened security measures in the South in view of the continued Soviet assistance to the North. Thus the security of the South, against communist designs became a matter of top priority along with the task of peaceful unification, and by March 1949 security forces of the South increased to about 114,000, of which 65,000 were army, 4,000 coast guard and 45,000 police. The total North Korean armed forces at that time were reportedly estimated at 24 divisions. Thus the years following the United Nations resolution witnessed more security and defence preparedness than an effective behavioural attitude for unification. The North continued to hold a hardened posture with repeated demands for the withdrawal of the United States armed forces from the South, which seemed to the South an unpracticable proposal in view of the defence preparedness of the North, a series of communist led armed revolts and guerilla attempts and the threats of the International Communist Movement.

The North Korean armed attack in 1950 created unprecedented mistrust and brought to the forefront the problems of national defence and security against forced armed occupation of the South by the North at any appropriate time. The North Korean attack caused intolerable damages in human lives and properties on both the sides; exposed the northern policy of subjugating the South by use of force; brought about a major deadlock in attempts for peaceful unification of the country, as well as posed fresh problems of national defence and security. The aggression caused an unprecedented alertness and preparedness to be able to defend their country south of the 38th parallel from any future surprise armed attack or possible subversive activities and provocations based on propaganda for a revolutionary upsurge. Besides, the war also sowed the seeds of deep mistrust and suspicion between the two opposing sides on the Korean peninsula, which made the efforts of unification more difficult.

Thus the conciliatory attempts and pathetic calls for unification resulted in a war, which vitiated an atmosphere of peace and good neighbourliness and initiated a new era of mistrust and suspicion. Besides, it also led to an active involvement of the two Super Powers in Korea for defending their own values, systems and thus the responsibility for active involvement and the presence of the United States forces in the South lies with the North—an issue on which the North has been grumbling repeatedly, has been reiterating the withdrawal of the U.S. armed forces as one of the pre-conditions for opening a dialogue with the South for 'peaceful unification'.

## The Geneva Conference, 1954

After the war, the convening of the Geneva Conference on April 26, 1954, on the problem of Korean unification, was an important landmark in the direction of establishing peace in the peninsula. The Armistice Agreement had recommended that a political conference of the powers involved should meet within three months to discuss and settle the questions of withdrawal of all foreign forces from Korea and the peaceful settlement of the Korean problem. It was a nineteen power conference—the six U.N. members, which had sent troops to Korea (with the exclusion of South Africa), the Republic of Korea D.P.R.K., P.R.C. and the U.S.S.R.

The 14-point proposal, put forward by the Republic of Korea, at the Geneva Conference of 1954, included the following:

1. With a view to establishing a united, independent, and democratic Korea, free elections shall be held under United Nations supervision in accordance with the previous United Nations resolutions relating thereto.

2. The elections shall be held in North Korea, where

such elections have not hitherto been possible, and in South Korea in accordance with the constitutional processes of the Republic of Korea.

3. The elections shall be held within six months from the adoption of the proposal.

4. Before, during, and after the elections, the United Nations personnel connected with the supervision of the elections shall enjoy full freedom of movement, speech, etc. to observe conditions and help to create a new atmosphere throughout the entire election area.

5. Before, during, and after the elections, candidates, their campaign helpers and their families, shall enjoy full freedom of movement, speech, etc. and other human rights which are recognized and protected in democratic countries.

6. The elections shall be conducted on the basis of secret ballot and universal adult suffrage.

7. Representation in the all-Korean legislature shall be proportionate to the population of the whole of Korea.

8. With a view to apportioning the numbers of representatives in exact proportion to population in the election areas, a census shall be taken under United Nations supervision.

9. The all-Korean legislature shall be convened in Seoul immediately after the elections.

10. The following questions, particularly, shall be left to the all-Korean legislature:

    (a) Whether the President of a unified Korea should be elected or not;

    (b) amendment of the existing constituion of the ROK;

    (c) disbandment of military units.

11. The existing constitution of the ROK shall remain in force except insofar as it may be amended by the all-Korean legislature.

12. The Chinese Communist troops shall complete their withdrawal one month in advance of the election date.

13. Withdrawal of the United Nations forces from Korea may start before the elections, but must not be com-

pleted until complete control over the whole of Korea is achieved and certified by the United Nations.

14. The territorial integrity and independence of the Unified, independent, and democratic Korea shall be guaranteed by the United Nations.

The resolution, relating to the above 14-points, caused a great flutter not only to the North Koreans but also the entire communist camp including the Soviet Union and China, and their immediate reaction to the resolution was hostile. Their arguments were that if the resolution containing the above proposals is accepted then it would subjugate North Korea to South Korea by 'imperialist' intervention. The delegate of the Soviet Union emphasised that the proposal containing the above 14 points resolution of South Korea was in contradiction with the actual situation in Korea and that it 'cannot serve as a basis for the decisions of the Geneva Conference'. The Chinese delegate, however, revised the earlier stand of North Korea in order to facilitate setting up of a supervisory commission of the neutral nations that had not earlier participated in the Korean War. The purpose of the setting up of this supervisory commission was to supervise the all-Korean elections. However, the functioning of the commission depended on a unanimous agreement between the South and the North. The delegate of South Korea as well as its Allies rejected the proposal with the contention that such a commission would prove to be worse than a communist veto. The Korean delegate also cited an example of a similar body that was earlier created to over-see the Korean Armistice in support of this contention.

It is significant here that at the Geneva Conference the stands taken by the South and the North, in order to resolve the conflict, were diametrically opposed to each other on three basic issues, namely, that—

(a)   the authority of the United Nations;
(b)   the principle of free elections; and
(c)   the withdrawal of foreign troops.

The South Korean stand was:

(a)   that the United Nations authority and competence in dealing with Korea should be recognised and the United Nations should have a primary role in bringing about a settlement;

(b)  a genuine and free Korean election should be held which should have a proportionate representation from South and North Korea; and

(c)  that the United Nations forces should continue to remain in Korea till the purpose of the mission of the United Nations is accomplished in a resolution of the Korean conflict by the creation of a unified, independent and democratic Korea.

The first and the third propositions of this proposal were totally rejected by the North as well as its Allies, the Soviet Union and China, and expressed their unhappiness over the second. The Soviet Foreign Minister Mr. Molotov vehemently denounced the United Nations intervention in Korea and called it as 'illegitimate' and alleged that it was designed solely 'to cover up the American aggression'. Mr. Molotov emphasised that the United Nations had turned 'belligerent' in Korea and thus it was without the capacity to act as an 'impartial international body'. The delegates from North Korea and China supported the contention of the Soviet delegate. In view of conflicting opinions and assertions from the South and North it became difficult to adopt a compromising attitude in the direction of establishing peace on the Korean peninsula. However, on June 15, 1954 the Allied group issued a '16-nation declaration on Korea' in which they formally acknowledged that the Geneva Conference did not prove to be fruitful in arriving at a reasonable conclusion to peacefully resolving the Korean conflict.

However, the North continued to exercise on the concept of revolution and communisation in the South and its attitude towards Korean unification, after the Geneva Conference, was based on advertising such conditions, as may be favourable to the communisation of the whole country in accordance with the Marxist-Leninist principles. This was confirmed at the Korean Workers' Party's Central Committee Meeting which was held on October 3, 1954. In this conference Kim Il Sung strongly denounced the American presence in South Korea and hoped that a revolutionary upsurge in the South may bring about a unification of the two parts. He stressed that until 'American imperialism', the major enemy of Korean unification, could be effectively isolated by revolutionary forces, the chances of unification were remote. In the meeting he called upon the Korean Workers' Party to consolidate itself in the North so as to be able to create a strong basis for the communisation of the entire peninsula, and to strive for long to achieve this goal.

The basic philosophy involved in the message of Kim Il Sung was that the North Korean attempts, in creating a revolutionary atmosphere in the Korean peninsula, would prove successful if the North was strong enough with rapid economic reconstruction. It is significant here that the emphasis on revolution by the North had been one of the important causes for creating a deadlock in the attempts for unification. According to Glenn D. Paige, this psychological warfare by the North, involved two basic tactics during this period. The first was that North Korea should be made economically and culturally attractive to the people living in the South, which they did by largely publicising the achievements during the post-Korean War economy plans. The second tactics adopted by the North related to the contact of political work in the South which included the infiltration of communist agents in the South by mixing with their relations in the South and trying to influence them with the achievements of the North in the direction of the well-being of the people.[52]

In response, the call put forward by Syngman Rhee of 'March North' was a rhetoric because Rhee fully acknowledged the impossibility of unifying the country, by military action and considered his idea as 'premature'.

It is significant that although Syngman Rhee admitted publicly that South Korea may not take unilateral action for peaceful unification, independent of American support, yet he did not part with the slogan 'March North'. Rhee believed that the slogan had an impact in boosting the morale of South Korea in their determination for unification, although he probably understood that South Korea was not militarily capable of carrying out a slogan. A second development in this regard is the 'United States–Republic of Korea Mutual Defence Treaty', which was signed on October 1, 1953, by which the South was committed not to take unilateral action against the North militarily. By this treaty the United States was committed to extend strategic assistance to the South in the event of an external armed attack.

Meanwhile, the Student Uprising of April 19, 1960 ended the First Republic on April 27, and caretaker government headed by Huh Chung adopted a cabinet system of government by making certain amendments in the constitution and discarding the presidential system. Accordingly, elections were held on July 29, 1960 and a Second Republic was established in August 1960.

John M. Chang was its first Premier. The North, however, took

advantage of the Student Uprising of April 19, 1960, to strengthen
its 'revolutionary line' for 'peaceful unification'. The theme of the
communist propaganda was the 'struggle of workers, peasants and
youths of South Korea against the U.S. imperialists' and wanted to
communicate to the southern citizens that it was the United States
which was responsible for these disturbances. The emphasis on the
withdrawal of the American troops from South Korea also
strengthened. It is noteworthy that the Student Uprising was reportedly directed against the rigging of the presidential elections but
the North availed it to its advantage. The North claimed, on April
21, 1960, that the Uprising was the struggle for resistance by South
Korean people and in an 'appeal to South Korean people' by the
Central Committee of the Korean Workers' Party called upon the
southern citizens to force the 'U.S. imperialist aggressor army' out
of South Korea.[53] The North gained some degree of self-
confidence at least from the fall of Syngman Rhee as the head of the
state.[54]

Such self-confidence on the part of the North was expressed in
the editorial of its party organ of May 5, 1960:

> 'Why is the people's living deteriorating steadily and the
> unemployed and foodless are increasing in the southern
> half which was liberated on the same day and at the same
> hour with the North? We don't know unemployment and
> poverty at all. The living standard of our people is rising
> every year ... These diametrically opposed facts come
> from the difference of systems, difference of policy and
> difference of leadership.'[55]

The South national unification was the central theme in the
campaign during the elections of July 1960 by different political
parties. The Socialist Mass Party held a position which was identical
with the Democratic Party, which was abandoning the slogan of
'March North' by Syngman Rhee and propagated resolving to
peaceful means for unification in accordance with the United Nations resolutions. The Socialist Mass Party declared that the national unification should be achieved through an all-Korean
election under the United Nations supervision and disapproved the fratricidal Korean War and advocated South-North
Korean cultural, economic and personnel exchange on a limited
scale. However, the July 1960 election gave a clear majority in
both the Houses to the conservative Democratic Party, which

secured 175 seats out of 233 in the Lower House and 31 out of 58 in the Upper House.

The position taken by the Chang government on the question of national unification was different from that of President Syngman Rhee's government. The Foreign Minister of the new cabinet declared, on August 24, that the new government would abandon the slogan of 'March North' and 'Unify' and soon after Premier Chang, in his first policy statement before the Lower House of the National Assembly, expressed his opinion on the unification policy that his government would adopt a different view from that of the former government. He laid emphasis on the holding of general elections throughout Korea under the supervision of the United Nations. His policy for unification may be summarised as follows:

1. Peaceful and democratic unification must be achieved by free elections in the South and the North, supervised by the United Nations.
2. The composition of the supervisory body for the election would be decided by a resolution of the U.N. members selected from U.N. member nations which have held free elections.
3. Establishment of a unified committee of South and North Korea before a national election would violate the U.N. resolution stating that the Republic of Korea is the sole legitimate government in Korea. Therefore, the proposal cannot be accepted.
4. Because there is no guarantee that the communist effort to destroy the Republic of Korea will be abandoned, any cultural and economic exchanges before reunification should be refused.
5. A unified Korea should be a state which preserves democracy and free civil rights. Neither a 'Red dictatorship', nor a 'White dictatorship' can be accepted.[56]

Though Premier Chang had specifically indicated that his policy would be different from that of the last government, yet this was not new emphasis, since an all-Korea election, under the supervision of the United Nations, was also reiterated by the Rhee government at the Geneva Conference and in the annual meeting of the United Nations General Assembly. What is most important is that the new government, in contrast with the former government, laid comparatively more emphasis on the issues of economic development than the issue of national unification. This shift in emphasis is very significant since the new government had visualised that a stronger South was more important so as to be able to defend itself against any possible northern attack, the economic development and stability to the people, living in the South, and hence a contrast in better living standards could be established, which was ultimately necessary for national unification.

With these objectives and new emphasis, Chang's Government initiated an ambitious programme known as the National Construction Service, which had two main objectives : (1) building social overhead capital and (2) unemployment relief. Besides, the Chang government also adopted a 5-year Economic Development Plan beginning in 1962.[57]

However, Chang's government continued to face the problem of the leftist movement, which was advocating the cause of Korean unification by the Koreans. During this period, the agitators, who demanded unification, were termed as 'progressives' and were divided into three groups : (1) the left reformists who represented the Socialist Mass Party and the Socialist Party; (2) the reformists who took a central position and who were represented by the Unification Socialist Party; and (3) the reformists who represented the right faction and who were represented by the Nationalist Unification Party. Although the factions had different views on the question of unification, yet there was consensus of opinion that the difficulties in the South relating to poverty and unemployment were due to the division of Korea.[58]

The important development during this period was the resolution adopted on November 1, 1960 by the Federation for National Unification, which was called 'Declaration of War' against the position of Chang's Government on unification. The Federation for National Unification was a progressive student organisation of the students of the department of political science at the Liberal Arts and Science College of Seoul National University. The resolution of the Federation stressed the following demands :

1. The older generation should assume full moral responsibility for the tragedy of the South-North division and should admit that they were not qualified to disregard or suppress the just utterances of the new generation on the unification issue.

2. All political parties and social organisations in South Korea must prepare themselves for an all-Korea general

      election in which they must compete with the communist party.

3. The government should resort to positive diplomacy based on the realities of the Korean situation. Premier Chang should visit the leaders of these two powers to explore the possibility of bringing about Korean unification.

4. Negotiation should begin immediately to implement one of the fundamental human rights, that is, the right of free correspondence between the South and North.[59]

However, the reaction of Premier Chang and his government to the proposal put forward by the federation, was discouraging and the Premier on January 6, 1961 rejected South-North Korean contacts of any kind. He emphasised that "national unification will be attained only when we have strengthened our democratic forces and won decisive victory in the general election throughout South and North Korea."

The North picked up these developments in the South and continued to report with emphasis American imperialism. In this regard the demands of the progressive faction among the students, which was emphasising a South-North dialogue, Kim Il Sung, on August 14, 1960, put forward his new unification policy in a speech at the 50th Anniversary of the 'Korean Liberation'. Kim Il Sung, in his new proposals accepted the demand for holding free elections throughout the North and South on a democratic basis without any external intervention and reiterated that if this was not acceptable to the Chang government, he was willing to settle for a confederation of fully autonomous North and South Korean governments on a provisional basis.[60] He said that a Supreme National Committee, coordinated by the representatives of the South and North Governments, could be established to coordinate such issues as cultural and economic development of the whole of Korea. He reiterated that for the time being the existing political system of both the North and the South would be maintained with free and independent activities guaranteed by the eventual unification of Korea. He also proposed a North-South exchange in the fields of science, culture, sports etc; but he specifically demanded the withdrawal of the American troops from the South and the reduction of the armed forces of both the North and South to one hundred thousand or less. These proposals of Kim Il Sung were continuously broadcast for several days.

The Chang government did not accept the proposal of Kim Il Sung and particularly his proposition of a confederation, and argued that the North wanted to be placed on an equal footing with the South and it is said that the fear on the part of the South at the time was probably its inferiority in the light of political consolidation and particularly economic development to North Korea.[61]

At this stage, we find a definite shift of emphasis in the attitude of North from the 'peaceful unification' to the 'Korean revolution'. The northern regime highlighted the anti-communist posture of the southern military government and in their broadcasts provoked the officers and men to rise in military coup and to overthrow the leadership. Besides the continued call for revolution in the South the North also entered into mutual defence treaties with the Soviet Union and China and replaced the Standing Committee of the party's Central Committee with the close confidants of President Kim Il Sung. Kim Il Sung visited Moscow and Peking and in seeking support for the North, entered into identical defence treaties with the two powers. According to these defence agreements, it was agreed that in the event of an armed attack, on the contracting parties, by a foreign power, the other party immediately would render all military and other assistance at its disposal. Similarly in a mutual defence agreement with China (July 11, 1961) a similar oath was taken that if any of the two parties is attacked by any state, the other party would render all military assistance.[62]

On the question of unification, Kim Il Sung emphasised that the ultimate goal of the North was the unification of Korea through a process of 'socialist revolution', which would take five stages.

## North Korean 'Federation' Proposal

While understanding the North Korean approach to 'peaceful unification', its strategy of 'federation' requires a little elaboration.

In its policy pronouncements for 'peaceful' unification of Korea, North Korea had proposed the concept of Korean federation ten times in three years from 1960 to 1963. In a speech on celebrating the fifteenth anniversary of Korean liberation, Kim Il Sung called for the creation of a 'confederated government' or 'Federation' between North and South Korea. He emphasised that North Korea was committed to the goal of setting up a unified Korean government under its own scheme and was willing to settle for a loose confederation of fully autonomous North and South Korean governments on a strictly provisional basis. He emphasised that a 'Supreme National Committee', organized by representatives of the two governments, would be established to coordinate such common state functions as 'cultural and economic development of the whole of Korea'. However, during this transitional period, he streesed, each side would maintain its own political system.

North Korean strong emphasis on a Korean Federation, during the 1960s, is also significant in view of Kim Il Sung's explanatory details of his 'peaceful' policy of unification—the realisation of which was based on five stages.[63]

The first stage was taken as a period of awakening of the South Korean people so that they could be easily mobilised for a revolutionary movement. It was said that the South Korean people were still taken in by the 'anticommunist' propaganda, which is a 'serious obstacle to the development of the revolution' in the South and 'must be removed by educating the people'[64]. The second stage was the 'regimentation of the main force of the South Korean revolution'. This was in consonance with Kim Il Sung's belief that 'owing to the absence of a political party of the working people, the South Korean people failed to gather the fruits of costly struggles in the past'.[65] The strategy behind this idea was the establishment of a 'revolutionary party guided by Marxism-Leninism and defending the broad interests of the broad masses'.[66] The third stage was the formation of a united front in order to build up a 'revolutionary party and closely uniting the workers and peasants and all other working people'.[67] The fourth stage was a positive action to expel the 'American Imperialists.'[68] And the fifth stage was the overthrow of all 'reactionary forces' in the South 'only by violent means'.[69]

From above, the 'revolutionary' character of the North Korean concept of Korean 'Federation' is evident, particularly, President Kim's 'united front' strategy of the 1940s, which he had adopted for consolidating his political power against his enemies in accordance with Marxist-Leninist principles. The concept of the United Front was repeated during the years of the proposal for a 'Federation', which gives a clue to the South to understand the kind of 'Federation' and the in-built strategy behind it. Professor Scalapino has given a brilliant analysis of the concept of the 'United Front' in the following words;

"The first step is the creation of a United Front, the development of a political milieu in which communist can interact with other forces on behalf of nationalist-reformist measures. The second step is the movement into action: the development of a 'peoples army', the 'unfolding of guerilla warfare tactics when the socio-political-economic climate is ripe.'[70]

Recently, North Korea put forward three 'pre-conditions' for the realisation of the federation plan, which are important to understand the latest North Korean concept of 'Federation'.

The three 'pre-conditions' include

(1) Non-recognition of the government of the Republic of Korea;
(2) Repeal of National Security Laws in South Korea; and
(3) Withdrawal of US armed forces from South Korea.

The above three 'pre-conditions' show the North Korean consistent approach to 'peaceful' unification. Thus the proposal for the establishment of a 'Federation' particularly the 'pre-conditions' only meant to the South as 'tactical occupation of South Korea by North Korea', and hence it was not acceptable to the South Koreans.

North Korean proposal of a Korean 'Federation' has often been understood to bear certain similarities with the North Vietnamese proposals put forward from time to time with the ultimate goal of communisation of South-Vietnam.

However, a strong contrast between the Koreans and the Vietnamese is that the South Korean people have experience of both the communist and republican regimes; the South Koreans have experienced the communist armed occupation, their administration during Korean War and the atrocities in the modus-operandi of the communists, till the North Korean attack was repulsed back by the United Nations Forces. In the present generation, it serves as a living memory with the majority of the people, in their developing confidence more for a 'Republican' rule than the 'Communist' rule, whereas the South Vietnamese people had never experienced the administration of the communists.

However, the North Korean concept of 'Korean Federation' appeared to the South more in consonance with post-Second World War pronouncements as federation, coalition, union and cooperation, which have been termed and analysed as meaningful strategies for communisation. As for North Korea, from the middle of 1960s. she began to adopt a 'hard line' on the unification issue which was probably provoked by the conclusion of the 'ROK—Japan Basic

Treaty', signed on June 22, 1965, which appeared to North Korea as a 'tripartite military alliance' between the United States, Japan and the Republic of Korea. The North continued to term it as an anti-communist alliance directed against it.

# THE SEARCH FOR UNIFICATION—II

The period beginning with the military coup from 1961 has been a very significant period for the South, since it was a period of political consolidation and economic modernisation. The new emphasis was important from a strategic point of view since it was believed that South could be able to defend herself against an apprehended encroachment from the North.

In the South, in May 1961, the Second Republic came to an end after only 9 months due to a military coup and the new government came into being with the establishment of the Supreme Council for National Reconstruction by 20 or more military leaders. The council had all legislative and judicial powers. However, after more than 2 years general elections were held and a new civilian government established a presidential and unicameral system. The era of President Park Chung Hee, who was re-elected in 1967 and 71, is very significant for the economic development of the South.

President Park held that the southern government was the only legal government and that North Korean regime was "an illegal territory of the Republic of Korea". This meant that the unification of Korea was "the recovery of the territory illegally occupied by an anti-state organisation opposed to the Republic of Korea". Similarly President Kim Il Sung also consistently holds that the northern government is the only legal government and that the 'southern clique' is an illegal government.

President Park's government, however, inaugurated an era of economic reconstruction in order to build up the South strong enough to 'defend itself against any possible armed attack from the North'. President Park was convinced that until and unless the national economic strength is 'comparatively stronger' than the North, discussion on unification may not bear any fruitful results. Thus the new government in the South embarked upon ambitious programmes of national economic development.

In view of the above, the Five Year Economic Development

Plan, in the South, paved the way for the National Reconstruction Movement. An Economic Planning Board was established and the First Five Year Plan was launched in January 1962 which aimed at increasing the GNP by 40.7% with an average annual increase of 7.1%. The First Five Year Plan laid emphasis on building up of the economic infrastructure and social overhead capital with an investment of about Dollar 2.5 billion. From January 1967, the Second Five Year Economic Development Plan was launched and both these plans showed a remarkable success in increasing the GNP growth rate which averaged more than 9%.[71]

Besides, the Nixon Doctrine which was for substantial reduction of American involvement in Asian regional affairs, also had its due impact on the shift in emphasis by President Park's government, laying more stress on national defence. In fact, this was primarily in deterrence of and in response to indications of political consolidation and economic construction by the North Korean regime, which had built up by 1960 an adequate socialistic revolutionary base required for the unification plan in accordance with their own principles.

The changing international political situation, with the beginning of 1970s, particularly the changes in the political dynamics in East Asia, created a new situation and this posed fresh challenges to various complicated political and strategic issues in the Asian region. The Soviet offensive of Collective Security System and the Sino-American rapprochement contributed to the emergence of Japanese militarism, which resulted in new emerging patterns of political relationships in East Asia (a detailed analysis and the implications of these factors have been given in a separate chapter) almost perplexed for sometime political observers and local governments. All these developments had their obvious impact on the political situation and foreign policy of South and North Korea as well as in their mutual relationship. Thus, the beginning of the 1970s is significant in the history of Korean unification not only because of the establishment of the Third Republic in South Korea, but also because during this period some understanding was achieved on the question of the Korean unification.

In 1972, there was a definite departure in the direction of unification. The beginning of normalisation between the United States and China which was initiated by the visit of Dr. Henry Kissinger to Peking had a definite impact on the bilateral relations of South and North Korea in the direction of their attempts for a peaceful unification. The meeting between President Nixon and Chou En-lai and their agreements on Korea, in February 1972, compelled the Koreans to take pragmatic steps in the direction of holding bilateral discussions for peaceful unification.

### President Park's August 1970 Proposal

President Park Chung Hhee, in his speech, on the occasion of the 25th anniversary of Korean Liberation, on August 15, 1970, declared that the government of the Republic of Korea was prepared to suggest the 'epochal and more realistic measures', with a view to removing, step by step, various artificial barriers existing between the South and the North, provided that North Korea was also 'equally sincere' in responding to his proposals. Some of the extracts from his speeches are given below:-

'No approach toward unification by peaceful means is feasible without the easing of tensions . . .

'As long as the North Korean communists persist in the type of aggressive and provocative acts in which they are now engaged, whatever they profess, it is nothing but a disguise, camouflage or fraud . . . .

'Therefore, such an approach should be preceded above all by an unequivocal expression of changed attitude by the North Korean communists, assuring the easing of tensions and followed by its implementation . . .

'Accordingly, the North Korean communists should desist forthwith from perpetrating all sorts of military provocations, including the dispatch of armed agents into the South, and make a public announcement that they henceforth renounce their policies for communising the whole of Korea by force and overthrowing the Republic of Korea by means of violent revolution. And they must prove their sincerity by deeds.

'If the North Korean communists accept and comply in deeds with the prerequisites and the United Nations clearly verifies this, I would be prepared to suggest epochal and more advanced measures with a view to removing, step by step, various artificial barriers existing between the South and the North, in the interest of laying the groundwork for unification and on the basis of humanitarian considerations.'[72]

Thus the South Korean President suggested that the North should desist forthwith from perpetrating all sorts of military provocations; to renounce their so called policies for communising the entire Korean peninsula 'by force' and to overthrow Southern Government with the help of 'violent revolution'; that this should be verified by the South with the help of the United Nations. President Park also suggested that the North should recognize the United Nations efforts for unified democratic and independent Korea and should also recognise the 'authority of the United Nations', then the South would not oppose North Korean presence in the United Nations and a discussion on the subject. But the North rejected President Park's proposals. However, President Park continued to emphasise that the South should develop the national strength till such time that the liberalisation process in North Korea can be internally advanced and ultimately directed in order to 'overwhelm the North Korean puppets in all areas.'

President Park's August 15 proposals are significant in the direction that South Korea had agreed not to oppose the simultaneous admission of South and North Korea into the United Nations.

## The Red Cross Talks 1972–1973

President of the Red Cross Society in the South Korea proposed to his northern counterpart that both the sides may negotiate the union of an estimated ten million families, which were separated for more than twenty years. He said that this was proposed strictly on the basis of non-political humanitarianism. Appreciably, there was an immediate response from the North Korean Red Cross Society approving the southern proposals, and on August 20, 1971, the representatives from both the sides started preliminary negotiations at the Neutral Nations Supervisory Commission office in Panmunjom. During the meetings, it was decided that the representatives of both South and North will hold full-fledged meetings in the southern and northern capitals alternately with a view to set up liaison offices. Both the sides, in October 1971, put forward their agenda items. During the period between August 1972 and July 1973, the two sides held a total of seven rounds of Full-dress SNRCC (South-North Red Cross Conference) meetings in Seoul and Pyongyang respectively. The South was represented by Bum Suk Lee, who is now the Minister for National Unification Board and the North was represented by Kim Tai-hi. However, from the beginning it began to be clear that the proposed humanitarian efforts in the inter-Korean talks had little chance of getting anywhere as the North Koran side was found more interested in using the talks as a forum for discussions on political problems than the agenda item itself'. The Northern insistence centred round repealing the Anti-Communist Law and National Security Law in the South. Notwithstanding, the Full-dress Red Cross Talks are significant to the extent that the talks provided the Northern and Southern delegation to see each other's life and society for the first time after the division of the country. The above Full-dress Red Cross Talks were in consequence of the signing of the South-North Joint Communique, on July 4, 1972, which was a dramatic outcome after the South-North contacts.

In May 1972, director of KCIA secretly visited Pyongyang and held talks with the North Korean President Kim Il Sung. The visit was turned later by the North by sending their second Vice Premier Pak Song Chol, who held discussions with President Park and the director of K.C.I.A. in Seoul.[73]

These 'secret' meetings, between the South and North, resulted consequently in the issue of a South-North Joint Communique on July 4, 1972. The Joint Communique included the following points:

(1)    unification shall be achieved through independent Korean efforts without subject to external imposition or interference;

(2)    the unification shall be achieved through peaceful means and not through the use of force against each other; and

(3)    as a homogeneous people, a broad national unity shall be sought above all, transcending difference in ideas, ideologies, and system.[74]

Besides the above three points, the two sides also concluded:

(1)    that in order to ease tension and foster an atmosphere of mutual trust between South and North, the two sides agreed not to slander or defame each other, not to undertake avowed provocations whether on a large or small scale and to take positive measures to prevent inadvertent military incidents;

(2)    that the two sides, in order to restore severed ties, promote mutual understanding and to expedite independent peaceful unification, have agreed to carry out various exchanges in many fields;

(3) that the two sides have agreed to cooperate peacefully with each other to seek early success of the South-North Red Cross Talks, which are under way with the fervent expectations of the entire people;

(4) that the two sides, in order to prevent the outbreak of unexpected military incidents and to deal directly, promptly and accurately with problems arising between south and north have agreed to instal a direct telephone line between Seoul and Pyongyang;

(5) that the two sides, in order to implement the aforementioned agreed items to solve various problems existing in the South and the North and to settle the unification problem on the basis of the agreed principles for unification of the fatherland, have agreed to establish and operate a South-North Coordinating Committee co-chaired by Director Lee Hu-rak and Director Kim Young-joo; and

(6) that the two sides, firmly convinced that the aforementioned agreed items correspond with the common aspirations of the entire people who are anxious to see an early unification of the fatherland and pledge before the entire Korean people that they will faithfully carry out these agreed items.

This Joint Communique was signed by Director Lee Hu-rak of the Central Intelligence Agency of Seoul with Director Kim Young-joo of the Organisation and Guidance Department of Pyongyang.[75] The Joint Communique is 'a phenomenal mark' in the history of South-North relations and unification. From political and strategic point of view and particularly from the point of view of establishing peace in the Korean peninsula, the Joint Communique of July 1972, is significant as an important landmark. This was a major peace offensive, strictly bilateral, and full of sincere feelings from both the sides and an attempt in solving the unresolved issue of unification. It was for the first time, in July 1972, that the two sides had sincerely sat across the table and expressed mutual confidence. The Joint Communique of July 4, 1972 had also its impact on the Full-Dress Red Cross Talks, that an immediate beginning was made next month for holding the sessions in Pyongyang and then in Seoul alternatively. However, the North Korean Red Cross insisted that the Red Cross be converted to a forum for discussions on the question of national unification arguing that there was no way of solving the problem of separated families, so long as the country remained divided. This point witnesses a shift in North Korean basic approach toward holding bilateral discussions on humanitarian issues by linking it with embarrassing political issues. Thus the last meeting was held in Pyongyang in July 1973, after which they refused to hold any further such meeting.

Besides, the environment of mutual confidence and optimism got a severe blow in the South when they discovered, with the help of the United Nations, the Northern strategic tunnel heading toward Seoul, which was believed to have been constructed for purposes of armed mobilisation from North to South. The discovery of the tunnel caused deep shock, suspicion and distrust in the minds of the Southern people.

Subsequently, South Korea offered the Four-Point Proposal in June 1973, and the substance of the proposal was that each of the two sides should open its society to the other side with a view to building a concrete foundation for mutual trust and understanding. The Four-Point Proposals offered by the South were as follows:

(1)   To observe July 4 South-North Joint Communique as a peace charter of the nation;

(2)   To make the humanitarian South-North Red Cross Talks successful as soon as possible in order to settle the problems regarding dispersed families in the South and North;

(3)   To inaugurate quickly the South-North Coordinating Committee's subcommittee; and

(4)   To inaugurate the SNCC's social-cultural subcommittee.

It was further elaborated by the South Korean co-chairman of the SNCC that the Economic Sub-committee was meant to facilitate the exchange of businessmen, scientific knowledge and materials, and also indicated that the social-cultural sub-committee would accelerate cultural exchanges, and a joint representation of the South and North sportsmen in international tournaments. He also suggested close coordination in the pursuance of knowledge regarding history, archaeology and other subjects and the exchange of newsmen and telegraph services. In these assertions, greater emphasis was laid on cultural exchanges and not on political matters with a view to first create an atmosphere of mutual trust and goodwill; and once this object was achieved, to discuss the political matters relating to the unification problem. This was in line with the approach that an atmosphere of goodwill, understanding and mutual trust is the primary requirement before taking up steps for national unification.

## President Park's Seven-Point Declaration

President Park Chung Hhee, put forward a Seven-Point Declaration for Peace and Unification on June 23, 1973 to facilitate the process of unification.

President Park's Seven-Point proposals were as follows:

(1) The peaceful unification of Korea is the supreme task of the Korean people and South Korea will continue to exert whole-heartedly for the accomplishment of this task;

(2) Between the South and North, there should be no interference in each other's internal affairs, nor the either side should commit aggression against the other:

(3) South Korea will continue to make efforts with all sincerity and patience;

(4) South Korea shall not oppose North Korea's participation with it in international organisations, if it is conducive to the easing of tension and the furtherance of international cooperation;

(5) South Korea shall not object to its admittance into the United Nations together with North Korea, if the majority of the member-states of the United Nations, provided that it does not cause hindrance to the cause of the national unification. Even before its admittance into United Nations as a member, South Korea shall not be opposed to North Korea also being invited at the time of the UN General Assembly's deliberations of the Korean question;

(6) The Republic of South Korea will open its door to all the nations of the world on the basis of reciprocity and equality. At the same time, South Korea urges those countries whose ideologies and social institutions are different to open their doors likewise to South Korea; and

(7)    Peace and good neighbourliness are the firm basis of the foreign policy of South Korea.[76]

## President Kim Il Sung's Five-Point Programme

President Kim Il Sung, in his speech at a mass meeting, during the visit of the general secretary of the Czechoslovak Communist Party, put forward the following Five-Point Programme for national unification:

(1)    To accept North Korea's Five-Point proposal of March 1973;

(2)    To realise many-sided collaboration and interchange between the South and North;

(3)    To convene a great national assembly composed of the representatives of people of all walks of life and the representatives of the political parties and social organisations in the South and the North to discuss and solve the reunification question;

(4)    To institute a South–North confederation under the single name of the Confederated Republic of Koryo; and

(5)    Not to enter the United Nations separately. If the South and the North want to enter the United Nations before unification, they should enter as one state at least under the name of the 'Confederation Republic of Koryo'.[77]

The proposals for national unification put forward by President Park Chung Hhee and Kim Il Sung on the same day accelerated mixed political reaction. President Kim Il Sung claimed that his Five-Point programme will remove misunderstanding and mistrust and that the present state of military confrontation would otherwise ultimately lead to war. The North Korean programme also implied, according to the North Korean reports American withdrawal from South Korea. Pyongyang believed that the United States presence in the South is a major hurdle in achieving the task of Korean unification. According to Kim Il Sung, American 'imperialism' supports the 'reactionary puppet clique' in Seoul and is opposed to the 'progressive and patriotie elements' in the South. He firmly believes that the withdrawal of US forces may be achieved through a fierce revolutionary struggle, based on three fronts, which include strengthening the North as a revolutionary base, reinforcing the revolutionary forces in the South, and inciting and supporting revolutionary struggle abroad against the United States.

President Park, soon afterwards explained his seven-point declaration, by emphasising the admission of South Korea and North Korea into the United Nations simultaneously. He believed that the joint entry of the South and North into the United Nations would help in minimising the tensions and re-establishing mutual trust and goodwill as well as it would help the Korean people enhance their national prestige. North Korea immediately rejected these proposals saying that the proposals contain a two Korea theory.

### Korean Question in the United Nations

The General Assembly of the United Nations in its 28th Session of September, 1973, discussed the two rival draft resolutions on Korean unification. One draft resolution co-sponsored by the United States, Great Britain and others proposed a dialogue between South and North Korea, suggested approval of the recommendations for the dissolution of the United Nations Commission for Unification and Rehabilitation of Korea and expressed the hope that the General Assembly may consider the membership of the South and North Korea in the United Nations for promoting the cause of peace and security in the peninsula heading towards achieving the goal of peaceful unification. The other resolution, which was co-sponsored by the Soviet Union, the People's Republic of China, Algeria and others, recommended the dissolution of the United Nations Commission for the Unification and Rehabilitation of Korea, held the annulment of the right to use the United Nations' flag by the foreign troops stationed in South Korea as well as the dissolution of the United Nations Command and also recommended the withdrawal of all foreign troops so that further steps could be taken in order to accelerate the peaceful unification of Korea.

From the above, it is clear that both the resolutions supported a continued dialogue between South and North Korea and the dissolution of the United Nations Commission for Unification and Rehabilitation of Korea. However, the rival assertions in the two resolutions included the question of the membership in the United Nations of South and North Korea, the future of the United Nations Command in Korea and the question of the withdrawal of foreign troops from South Korea. There was heated discussion on the subject which continued for as long as five days.

North Korea, which had participated for the first time in the United Nations General Assembly debate, emphasised that North Korea had always aspired for peaceful and independent resolution of the Korean conflict and held that the root cause of the conflict was the occupation of South Korea by foreign troops which was the source of interference in their internal affairs. The North Korean delegate also reiterated strongly that the question of the simultaneous membership of the United Nations by both South and North Korea was an imperialist old method of divide and rule for colonial domination. With regard to the United Nations Command, the Northern delegate held that it was established in violation of the United Nations principles from the very beginning and that US troops are stationed there in the guise of the United Nations Command. The Northern delegate asked 'why should the United States Army continue to enjoy the sign-board of the United Nations forces'.

The South Korean delegate alleged that the North Koreans have never changed their strategic objective of communising South Korea and urged North Korea to completely depart with this attitude and come to the conference table for dialogue. He emphasised the necessity of the presence of the United Nations Command stating that this body in Korea by virtue of the Security Council resolution and our wholehearted consent, is for the sole purpose of maintaining peace and security, and that its dissolution would make the armistice agreement null and void. On the question of withdrawal of foreign troops from South Korea, the Seoul delegate held that the stationing of foreign troops has been done by mutual agreement on the request of South Korea and the subject falls within the juridsdiction of the countries concerned. As for the South-North representation in the United Nations, he argued that this is important and in no way jeopardises the efforts for unification of Korea. In view of the rival assertions, it became difficult to arrive at a compromise conclusion. However, Dr. Henry Kissenger's meeting with Chou En-lai, on November 21, 1973, called for a continued dialogue between South and North Korea to achieve the goal of peaceful unification. It ignored the North Korean proposal for the disbandment of the United Nations Command and endorsed the **military** status quo in Korea.

### President Park's Proposal, January 1974

President Park proposed, on January 18, 1974, a non-aggression pact for 'peaceful co-existence' between the South and North until the goal of unification was achieved in an atmosphere of mutual goodwill and trust which had been a preliminary requirement of any positive steps to be taken for Korean unification. President Park proposed that:

(1)   both the sides shall announce to the world never to wage armed aggression against one another;

(2)   both the sides shall refrain from mutual interference in the internal affairs of the other side; and

(3)   under any circumstances, the existing armistice agreement shall remain effective.

President Park reiterated that 'if these principles are observed, peace will come to the Korean peninsula, and if North Koreans have no intention to abide by them, any agreement would be rendered useless'.[78]

North Korea, however, rejected the above proposal and called it a design to freeze two Koreas permanently, further the national division, and perpetuate US occupation in South Korea. The dismissal of the proposal which came in an editorial of North Korean News Paper Nodong Sinmun, also charged that there was no indication in the proposal for the withdrawal of the United States troops. The editorial contended that the proposal relating to non-aggression agreement was to keep separately questions of 'peace' and 'peaceful unification'. In regard to the question of peaceful co-existence, the editorial held that it was a concept that related the two independent sovereign states.

### President Kim II Sung's March 1974 Proposal

A significant proposal was put forward by North Korea to the United States on March 25, 1974 with the motivation of concluding a peace agreement with the United States. The proposal was sent in a letter to the United States Congress adopted at the third session of the Supreme Peoples Assembly. The proposal contained emphasis on the following points:

(1)   The existing armistice agreement is an agreement on 'military armistice' and thus does not guarantee peace;

(2)   The existing armistice agreement has in itself become outdated and hence does not conform to reality;

(3)   North Korea has come to realise its meaninglessness to discuss the question of military confrontation or the conclusion of a peace agreement with South Korea; and

(4)   If the existing armistice agreement is to be replaced with a peace agreement, it is right and proper to settle the question with the United States, which holds the real power and had signed the armistice agreement;[79]

However, a vigorous call was made simultaneously for the withdrawal of the American forces at the earliest possible date.

The motivations for indirectly contacting the United States Congress were that—

(1)   North Korea wanted a vigorous and free debate in the United States Legislature with a view to put pressure on the US administration to reconsider the decision of the continued presence of the United States forces in South Korea;

(2)   to provoke and invigorate opposition in the United States Legislature, against the Treasury Benches for opening dialogue with the Soviet Union and China on the Korean question and to discuss the possibility of the withdrawal of American troops from Korea in view of the increasing doctrine and changed political situation power in East Asia;

(3)   to find out, from among the opposition on Treasury Benches, the individual leaders who have sympathy for the North Korean cause so that in course of time they may be cultivated suitably to champion the North Korean stand in the US Senate and the House of Representatives; and

(4)   another reason was to put the issue for discussion within and outside the Legislature including the American press, the American intelligentsia and the American masses and to extract sympathies for North Korean cause, since in this new modus operandi the United States citizens may feel inclined to discuss and

sympathise with the North Korean cause, as it was North Korea which had voluntarily approached the United States directly and sought help in resolving the existing conflict.

Hence it was under the above motivations that North Korea approached the United States and expected a favourable response at least from a small section of American society comprising legislators, policy makers and the intelligentsia.

However, the response in the United States was not satisfactory. Washington turned down the proposals and maintained that the Korean problems must be solved directly by Seoul and Pyongyang.

### President Park's August 1974 Proposal

Some more significant proposals for peaceful unification were put forward, on August 15, 1974, by President Park Chung Hhee, his commemorative address on the 29th anniversary of National Liberation, in which he proposed "Three Basic Principles for Peaceful Unification", which have been stressed enough by the South in successive years. These basic principles were as follows:

(1)  "Peace should be firmly established on the Korean peninsula. For this a mutual non-aggression agreement should be concluded between the South and the North;

(2)  "the South and the North should open their doors to each other and mutual trust should be built between them. For this purpose, they should pursue rapid progress of the South-North dialogue with sincerity, and many-sided exchanges and cooperation should take place between them; and

(3)  "Based on the above foundations free general elections should be held throughout Korea under fair election management and supervision, and in direct proportion to the indigenous population, thereby achieving the unification of the country."[80]

President Park's proposal that an all-Korea election, in direct proportion to the indigenous population, is significant, since it proposed unification not by negotiations, but by involving the people as a whole.

The three infiltration tunnels along the Demilitarised zone, however, jolted the masses of people in the South. Besides these three tunnels, several other tunnels were also believed to have been constructed by the North in view of her 'strategic design' on the South. All these tunnels were heading to Seoul. In 1975, North Korean President made trips to Rumania, Algeria, Mauritania, Bulgaria, Yugoslavia and Peking, which were intended to win fresh support from these countries. This accelerated a demand in South Korea to strengthen her defence and national security. There were mass rallies in support of national defence throughout South Korea and the South Korean National Assembly passed a resolution warning the North that any aggression would be vehemently repulsed. The United States also renewed its pledge of support to South Korea emphasising the strategic importance of the Korean peninsula.

President Park Chung Hhee, again on July 4, 1975, on the occasion of the anniversary of the Joint Communique stressed that "North Koreans should accept the authority and competence of the United Nations and that they should immediately terminate their preparation for aggressive war, all acts of indirect aggression, and self-destructive acts of disgracing their own nation in international society" and urged them "to normalise the suspended South-North dialogue by requesting the resumption of the full-fledged meetings of the South-North Coordinating Committee and South-North Red Cross Conference respectively at the earliest possible date."

The question of 'Korean Unification' was again discussed by the UN First Committee on October 21, 1975. It was placed on the agenda as item No. 119, which was divided into two parts—

(1)  creation of favourable conditions for converting their armistice into durable peace in Korea and accelerating their independent and peaceful reunification of Korea; and

(2)  urgent need to implement fully the consensus of the 28th Session of the General Assembly on the Korean question and to maintain peace and security on the Korean peninsula.

Number 1 was a pro-North Korean draft resolution and number 2 was a pro-South Korean draft resolution. The two draft proposals, however, recommended the need to dissolve the United Nations Command and to work out an alternate arrangement through negotiations. However, on October 30, both the conflicting draft resolutions were adopted with 59-51 votes and 29 abstentions for the Western draft, and 51-38 votes and 50 abstentions for the communist draft. The General Assembly rectified the decisions of the First Committee on November 18, 1975. Thus, one more effort in the United Nations General Assembly failed to bring out a constructive solution for the unification of Korea.

Again in 1976, the Korean question figured in the UN General Assembly Session in which North Korean supporters proposed a resolution calling for the removal of foreign troops. But in deterrence of losing sufficient support for their resolution, in view of more effective counter-moves from the Western bloc, the North Korean supporters withdrew their proposal. Thereafter the counter-proposal by the U.S. and Japan was also withdrawn. It was generally believed that the Korean question may preferably be discussed bilaterally instead of bringing it to international forums—an attitude which was in consonance with the South Korean policy.

President Park Chung Hhee who deserves the credit for this surprising achievement in terms of industrialisation and economic development has been the founding pillar of the South Korean development strategy. It is with this grand economic strategy that South Korea now feels more confident and powerful in her dealings. But a deadlock in the see-saw continues to exist with allegations and counter-allegations. The basic approach to be adopted, methodology to be discussed and, observations to be made on the question of exploring attempts for peaceful unification in accordance with the Joint Communique still remain an open question.

### Some Economic Aspects

It is very significant that in the bilateral exercises on 'peaceful' unification, from both the sides, an important, though inadvertent, outcome has been the development of the economy of both the North and South; and the statistics speak of a much better standard of achievements in growth rate, if compared to international standards and other developing countries of the world. A strong economic base was thought important as a strategy for comparative show of strength, in terms of justifying either of the two ideological systems as a better system than the other, for the well-being of the people and a welfare state.

While Germany is an example in the European context, the Korean peninsula is a brilliant example in Asia for understanding the so called 'proletarian' and 'capitalist' systems.

During the Japanese rule, industrial development was mainly concentrated in the North, which contained most of the natural resources including major mineral deposits. Thus after liberation and bifurcation, the South found itself at a marked disadvantage in industrial development and had to take up afresh industrialisation and economic growth.

The economies of North and South are based on two different systems, i.e., a state-controlled planned socialist economy in the North and a competitive free market economy in South Korea, which means that the concepts of national income are different in the two halves.

In the Korean context, particularly, the comparative statistics between per Capita GNP in North and South Korea hardly indicate actual per Capita consumption especially due to differences in military expenditures and gross investment rates of the two different economic systems. Much more important become the 'restrictions' which are usually imposed by the method of comparative economic systems, particularly the differences in the respective concepts of national income, the announced figures for national income and the actual performance—all this makes it very difficult to arrive at a reasonably accurate conclusion of superiority or inferiority of one over another. It is well understood that the primary function of the economic activity and the labour concept of an individual is to earn profits for national growth and better standards of living. In the 'capitalist' countries, it is done mostly on individual free competition basis, whereas in the totalitarian states it is totally controlled by state initiatives and conflicts have existed between the planning body and the production units in China and the Soviet Union and the East European countries, the most recent being the Poland example.

The North Korean economic development has emphasised from the beginning, on heavy industry. In heavy industry, the stress has been on metal, machine and power industries, with a view that the development of heavy industry would result in the production of enough capital goods for the subsequent development of light industry, agriculture and defence production.

The management of heavy industry was put under central authorities and that of light industry under the provincial authorities for the purpose of better coordination between the two sectors for effective performance. In regard to the agricultural development, North Korea has put emphasis on the production of major grains and industrial raw materials under four movements—irrigation movement, electrification movement, mechanisation movement and use-chemical movement. Thus the basic objective has been to establish a self-sufficient economy through the priority development of heavy industry that will in turn help develop light industry and agriculture. The emphasis on heavy industry, however, corresponds to the Marxist ideology of putting emphasis on the production of machinery, which shall form the basis for the material and technical development of the society. Moreover, the stress on heavy industry was also tuned to maintain military superiority over South Korea.

South Korea also embarked on a programme of massive economic reconstruction and modernisation as a priority task to achieve the national goal of peaceful unification.

President Park had repeatedly stressed that "the only way to national re-unification is through economic reconstruction and prosperity as is the case with West Germany"[81] and "our basic principle for unification is to foster our strength by expediting economic construction and modernising our country to the level of advanced nations as rapidly as possible"[82]

In view of the above, South Korea has been trying to expand external economic cooperation and trade as a major policy since the 1960s. The South has also been trying to form economic ties with non-hostile 'socialist' countries since the early 1970s by fully separating political considerations from economic affairs. Even possible trade with China and Soviet Union was talked about in Seoul.

South Korea's First Five Year Economic Plan (1962–66) laid emphasis on the development of energy resources; key industries i.e. fertilizer and iron and steel; social overhead capital i.e. railroads, ports and communications; export industries, import substitution industries and agricultural production. The Second Five Year Plan (1967–71) emphasised electronics, the petro-chemical industry, exports and increased income for agricultural households. The Third Five Year Plan made continued efforts to develop heavy industry i.e. iron and steel, ship-building and machinery and overall development of land, development in science and technology and the New Community Movement. The Fourth Five Year Plan concentrated on maintaining a favourable balance of payments by enlarging trade volume, reducing dependence on foreign sources for investment, improving the industrial sector and achieving equity in living standards. Besides all this several other programs have been introduced to develop technology, higher effciency and a better international standard.

On the question of foreign trade, South Korean trade volume was five times inferior to North Korea in 1960. But South Korea caught up an exceeded North Korea 15 times in 1978.

On trade deficit, North Korean trade deficit is relatively larger than that of South Korea, although both suffer trade imbalances.

In iron and steel, in 1979, South Korea had a production capacity of 8,390,000 tonnes. In the field of Ship-building, South Korea holds international reputation and she is placed third in the world. Similarly in electronic products, South Korea is able to meet both export and domestic needs through mass production and advanced technology of international standards, whereas North Korea produces only for domestic use.[83]

The Southern strategy for industrial development revolves around substantial fiscal support, private initiative strongly supported by various government measures, expansion of social overhead capital investment for smooth flow of economic activity, rapid export expansion particularly of manufactured goods, a much improved balance of payments policy including flow of foreign capital into productive investments in order to make rapid economic changes in both internal and external sectors.

Economic key indicators suggest that by 1991 South Korea will rank as one of the 20 biggest economic powers in the world and as one of the first twelve leading trading nations of the world. It is believed that from its present status as a semi-industrialised middle-income nation, it will have been transformed into an advanced industrial nation with its per capita GNP reaching approximately to 1975 levels of Japan and Western Europe.

In view of North and South comparative economic achievements, as they stand today, the statement of President Kim Il Sung in 1960 is interesting in which he attributes the backwardness of South Korean economy to the 'difference of systems, difference of policy and difference of leadership.'[84] Now, in spite of more than double the population, the South Korean economy witnesses a tremendous achievement, not only in terms of North-South comparison, but her growth rate is comparable to that of the most advanced countries of the world and thus in view of the above statement it itself clarifies the leadership capabilities. This is an important factor that North Korea has been 'all the more hesitant to open channels or communication to the outside world or to allow their people access to uncontrolled information', which has been the 'contrasting performance of the two economies over the decade of the 1970s'.[85] It is evident that 'by almost every standard of measurement—per capita income, growth rates, social programmes, amenities for modernisation—South Korea moved into a commanding lead over the rival regime in the North during the 1970s'.[86]

# THE SEARCH FOR UNIFICATION—III

## President Chun Doo Hwan's Proposals

Recently an attempt was made by South Korean President Chun Doo Hwan, in January 1981, based on the internationally accepted behavioral norms of 'bilateralism', inviting North Korean President Kim Il Sung "to visit Seoul without any condition attached and free of any obligation on his part" and has ensured that he "will extend all possible cooperation to him if he wishes to travel to any place of his choice in order to take first-hand look at the actual situation in Seoul, other cities, or rural areas".[87]

President Chun Doo Hwan has also proposed that "I also want to make it clear that I am prepared, at any time, to visit North Korea, if he invites me on the same terms as I offer". President Chun Doo Hwan also "solemnly" reiterated that "the highest authorities in the South and North exchange visits" with a view to provide an opportunity to restore a sense of trust between the two sides 'to preclude a recurrence of tragic fratricidal war', offering a movement to unconditionally resume the suspended dialogue to open the way for peaceful unification. Through this proposal, Chun has exhibited tremendous confidence and personal conviction that an avenue to the solution of any arising or pending problems, between the two sides, can be found if only "we steadfastly work to narrow our differences".[88] He emphasised that "the path of unification is not paved by unilateral proposals rich only in rhetoric, nor by written promises that are not kept; it is paved by restoration of trust."[89]

In view of his pragmatic understanding and approach to the problem of unification, in the reality of the situation, he stressed that "a fratricidal war, deepening national heterogeneity, strife in the international arena, and intermittent dialogue are but a few exam-

ples of the many spiritual and material wounds inflicted upon us by
the territorial partitioning" and thus "we have no use for empty
agreements, which without embodying the will to translate them
into action are not worth the paper they are written on. What is
truly needed is a firm resolve on both sides to honour even the
smallest agreement already reached".[90] While recognising that
"both sides have consistently engaged in a war of words and vain
expositions of unilateral proposals", he complained against the
North Korean "scheme to communise the entire Korean peninsula",
but simultaneously expressed confidence in the "iron clad security of
the ROK Armed Forces and the firm resolve of the people to defend
their country, which is growing steadily stronger."[91]

The New Year Policy Statement, containing the above proposal
on South-North relations, also stressed priorities on an independent
diplomacy and self-reliant defence; developing closer relations with
the United States, Japan and other friendly nations under the principles of mutual understanding and respect; improvement of relations
with 'non-hostile communist countries as well as with the non-
aligned countries' irrespective of different ideological and socio-
political systems.[92] Again, on June 5, 1981, South Korean President,
Chun Doo Hwan, in an address at the inaugural session of the
Advisory Council on Peaceful Unification Policy, proposed to North
Korea, a meeting between the highest authorities of the South and
North. President Chun Doo Hwan's June 5 offer suggested that he
and Kim Il Sung meet at any time and any place to discuss frankly all
questions raised by both sides, including the proposed exchange of
visits and both South and North Korean Unification formulae. President Chun Doo Hwan, in the June 5 proposals, also advocated that
'both South and North Korean authorities open their societies to the
entire Korean people who have the right to make decisions concerning unification'.

The June 5 Proposals suggested involvement of the people of
the South and North to decide their destiny with the emphasis that
'the people of the two zones of Korea ought to be allowed to decide
on the system for a unified fatherland.' The people-to-people approach also included exchange in athletic, cultural, academic, postal
and economic fields. Thus, the June 5 proposal evidences an open
door policy and approach by suggesting that the proposed meeting
discuss all the issues raised so far between the two sides, which shows
Seoul's resolve to tackle the unification issue affirmatively.

As is well known to the present generation, the conflict has involved bitter experiences of fratricidal war, allegations and counter-allegations, mistrust and hatred, ideological compulsions and contradictions, misinformation and lack of proper appreciation and understanding, and regimented discipline and society. There is also the much apprehended lurking danger of another war at the 38th parallel and mutual awareness of the consequences, all the more so in view of the well-known Super Powers' global game in mutual defence of their respective foreign policy interests.

Besides above, other peace instruments like discussions in the United Nations General Assembly and the Security Council, a tripartite international conference, consisting of South Korea, North Korea and the United States, as well as propositions at the non-aligned forums have all failed to come to a conceivable, comfortable and mutually agreed-upon formula due to the overriding political, ideological, strategic fundamental interests of the Super Powers—the well-known international custodians of both the outbreak of hostilities as well as the resolution of peace and conflict, whether bilateral, regional or international in character. In the past, the peace efforts, whether bilateral or through a regional or international apparatus, have been marred by the international community, because of the highly sensitive nature of the conflict. singular in the Asian context. The conflict evidences a sharp contrast in approaches and dimensions, and in the event of open violence at the 38th parallel the conflict risks an open confrontation between the two Super Powers in defence of their much-preserved ideological and strategic interests.

In view of the above political and strategic situation the only option open for resolving the Korean conflict seems to be through 'bilateralism'.

In this context it has to be understood properly that 'bilateralism' or bilateral negotiations have been accepted and acknowledged as the most important instrument for the peaceful resolution of conflicts, in contrast to violence or war which has been universally disapproved and acknowledged as unlawful for resolving a conflict. The post-World-War II history evidences that during prolonged wars bilateral peace negotiations have formed the core of mechanics of the resolution of the conflicts. Thus in accordance with the internationally accepted peace concept of bilateralism the 'January 12 proposal' envisaging a meeting of two heads of states seems a step forward in the direction of peaceful resolution of the conflict.

The decision seems to have been taken in view of the realities of the situation, compulsions and the operational mechanics of the governing forces involved in the conflict. Much more, the decision to propose the meeting of the two heads of states, taken by the South Korean President Chun Doo Hwan, at a time and place convenient to North Korean President Kim Il Sung also speaks of enormous confidence and great optimism—the two important pre-requisites, which are needed for the resolution of the conflict. An invitation extended to his North Korean counterpart to visit Seoul is convincingly the most practical approach in order to enable the North Korean head to apprise himself of the economic and social advancement of the people in a free, democratic and changing government-system. An experience to live in a city of sprawling sky-scrapers, bustling business environment and a developed rural base may all possibly look mythical against the dogmatic nineteenth century concept of Marxism, which has become more or less irrelevant among developed societies in the late twentieth century. The fact that the offer has been put forward without any 'preconditions'—speaks of and attests to the sincerity in approach in at least making a beginning in the direction of a peaceful resolution of the conflict.

Thus, in a bilateral as well as an international framework, the offer, as embodied in the above proposal, is a definite departure from the previous efforts; and in the absence of any 'pre-conditions' is a passionate expression full of fraternal sentiments and optimism. Although North Korea has initially rejected the offer by calling it 'hypocritical' it enjoys the sanctity of UN Charter, within the well-accepted norms of international behaviour.

Besides the above proposal, Bum Suk Lee, the Minister for National Unification Board also made a fervent appeal, with an invitation to the northern authorities, to establish contact and discuss complete procedures for the meeting. Lee emphasised that " all the problems pending between the South and North can be solved, if only the highest authorities of the two halves realise the proposed mutual visits and strive with patience to reduce their differences of opinion." This was due to the fact that, as Bum Suk Lee observed, previous attempts to conduct a South-North dialogue in various channels were unsuccessful because of a lack of mutual trust and a few agreements, actually arrived at, were in principle only. Bum Suk Lee said that the territorial division of Korea has persisted for 36 years matching the length of the Japanese colonial rule and thus " the government headed by President Chun Doo Hwan will continue to concentrate on restoring mutual trust and goodwill, which has been a constant policy of the Republic of Korea on the question of peaceful unification." Bum Suk Lee observed, that he would prefer to call the unification matter a 'policy' than a 'strategy', with a view to express the South's 'ardent desire and optimism for peaceful unification. These proposals put forward by Seoul do not reflect any change in the traditional South Korean policy of peaceful unification. They accept the historical realities that the people of Korea have lived in a divided land under different ideologies, ideals and political systems for nearly four decades, and the proposed meeting between the two heads of states may lead to a beginning to help develop a new climate for mutual understanding, which is a major necessity at this stage of a protracted deadlock. After all, somehow a beginning has to be made either bilaterally or internationally. As discussed earlier, bilateral efforts are considered to be more positive and pragmatic than international efforts, since international efforts directly implicate some pulls and pressures due to rival interests. Thus President Chun Doo Hwan's proposals for a handshake, without any preconditions, may positively help ease tension, to some extent, which is an important prerequisite for any constructive and worthwhile attempt for the realisation of the ultimate settlement.

At this point it is significant to remember that the examples of normalised relations between East and West Germany, Egypt and Israel, India and Pakistan have demonstrated that regardless of how deep the disputes may be, a dramatic breakthrough has resulted from a mutual trust created by an exchange of visits between the highest authorities. The Israel-Egypt dispute matches approximately the same length of time as the Korean conflict and the Camp David meeting between the two leaders of the two countries was definitely a positive attempt to help ease tension between the two states in the direction of ultimate resolution of the conflict. The Camp David agreement is an example where the two states, realising their unwelcome confrontation under international pressures, have adopted the path of bilateralism in normalising their long, hostile relations. Moreover, it also demonstrates a positive attempt and answers a major question whether two confronting states have to adopt an approach towards normalisation in accordance with their own national interests or in accordance with the interests of the two Super Powers.

Thirdly, it also amply demonstrates that the longstanding disputes, between two hostile states can be solved through utilising only the good offices of one Super Power whose efforts, terms and conditions are more conciliatory, accommodative and in the interest of the two confronting States, and disregarding the other if necessary. In the context of Super Power conflict, the Camp David agreement was a master-stroke of US foreign policy in the 1970s, particularly of Dr. Brzezinski's hard bargaining exercises.

The follow-up of Israel-Egypt accord also demonstrates that mutual trust can be created by exchange of visits between the highest authorities. Thus, in the Korean context, a meeting of the two heads of states could be followed by exchange of visits by high authorities, which may help develop a new climate of mutual understanding, a fundamental pre-requisite in the attempts for the realisation of the ultimate goal of national unification by peaceful means.

# CHAPTER VI

# CONCLUSION

The Korean conflict is very much absorbed within the inter-twined texture of the Super Power conflict and is to be understood within the in-built mechanics of the dilapidated political and strategic infrastructure of the two Super Powers in the triangularity of their relationship with China. The rich analytical contributions on East Asian political dynamics, offered by some learned and eminent academics like Professor Richard L. Walker, Professor Robert A. Scalapino, during the last three decades, are particularly relevant in understanding an objective view of compulsions and cross-currents involved in the Korean conflict. Therefore, the genesis of the Korean conflict is to be traced not to the dilapidated political and factional infrastructure of Korea, after the Japanese surrender in 1945, but to the hegemonic framework of the Super Powers after the Second World War.

The unfortunate division of the country at the 38th parallel, which ensued an era of conflict on the Korean peninsula, may be taken as an attempt on the part of the two Super Powers to establish their global hegemony in the ruins of Second World War. The newly liberated states, which wanted peace and a popular responsible government, however, suffered from an in-built disadvantage of 'factionalism' within the leadership, which led the international custodians of democracy to believe that there may emerge a state of 'civil war' or that the local situation did not warrant the establishment of a popular and responsible government. Besides, the period, soon after the Japanese surrender, was a period of chaos and confusion and provided a fertile opportunity to Kremlin leaders to baptise, as large sections of society as possible, with the Marxist ideology, under the so called International Communist Movement. Thus

104

the communist occupation of China, North Korea, North Vietnam and the East European states, basically on grounds of strategic considerations, ultimately turned out to be political and has posed a major threat to the governments based on free will and aspirations of the people in Asia and Europe.

A pragmatic analysis and assessment of the Korean conflict suffers from an increasingly marked contrast that exists today between North and South. While the North has a closed and unicentered society under the personality cult of 'an ageing autocrat', and the people suffer from a mechanical discipline and uniformity in attitude, expression, thought and way of life, the South has been an open society, with wide international contacts at global level and the masses of people have witnessed free elections and expression of their will in running the government.

The issue of 'unification' rather a 'peaceful unification' of the two halves of the country is the most important problem of the Korean conflict. The issue, which is basically a bilateral one in character, suffers, however, from certain compulsions particularly of the International Communist Movement, which do not fit in accordance with the will and aspirations of the majority of the Korean people. It is a problem of political and strategic mechanics of totalitarian expansionism on the one hand and the defence of freedom and democracy, human rights and improved economy on the other.

In order to overcome mistrust and suspicion, a pragmatic and realistic approach and an attitude of conciliation and confidence may be helpful in gradually eliminating obstacles that stand in the way of achieving unification in order to overcome the misunderstanding caused by long period of separation. With the help of bilateral dialogue at the highest level, the fear of another war of forcible occupation and the existing environment of suspicion may be gradually eliminated from the minds of the Koreans, which may help them develop an attitude of trust and goodwill. This could possibly be achieved with the conclusion of mutual non-aggression treaty between the South and North in a meeting of the two heads of states. This could possibly be followed with the exchange of personnel and cooperation in economic, cultural, educational and other fields between the two halves. Besides, taking into consideration the view of the people of the whole peninsula may be a basic necessity to ensure a just and fair unification, for, if the people are taken into confidence at different stages, the outcome may be conciliatory and acceptable.

The people of Korea have every reason to aspire for unification and lasting peace in view of the fact that they have been under the imperial domination or subjugation for a long period of time. Due to the geographical situation, they have been the target of colonial domination and exploitation by one or the other neighbouring power in the past.

Then comes the important question of establishing regular contacts between the South and the North with a view to create an atmosphere of mutual goodwill and trust as a pre-requisite in the attempts for unification and the recalcitrant attitude on the part of the offending leaders in making an appreciable response. The promotion of a cordial atmosphere between the conflicting states has always been considered, in history, as an essential pre-requisite in the gradual process of winning mutual confidence. The memories of the Korean War are still alive in the political and social psychology of those who fought it.

In view of this, the South has often extended alternate proposals during the last three decades and the latest one has been President Chun Doo Hwan's proposal of holding a meeting of the heads of the Southern and Northern governments at a place and time convenient to the North. But the North has turned down the proposals calling them 'hypocritical' and continues to harp on the 'confederation' system and the withdrawal of foreign troops. However, in view of the experiences of the war of 1950–53 and particularly the discovery of the tunnels heading towards the Southern capital, the South insists on the conclusion of a 'non-aggression' pact initially to ensure mutual security interests.

Out of the problematic issues that are involved in the study of the Korean conflict, the most embarrassing for the communist society is that South Korea represents an example in terms of economic progress, vis-a-vis its communist counterpart of North Korea. The ever increasing contrast in the well-being of the people, makes the Marxist society and its leadership to suffer from an 'inferiority complex' and raises doubts on the usefulness of the very basic Marxist philosophy for the development cause. The leadership advocating that philosophy fears its people being exposed to the open world of economic prosperity and basic human rights and freedoms, lest it may give rise to counter-revolution and the people may aspire for the material comforts of South Korea. The priority put on the economic development by both North and South, as a means of strengthening their respective bases has been considered as a strategic pre-requisite in achieving the goal of national unification. But the net outcome in the economic powergame is evidenced by their comparative GNP that South is boasting four times more GNP than the North. It is particularly more significant since the South has more than double the population and less natural resources than the North.

North Korea is a 'neighbouring socialist state' of both China and the Soviet Union, but geographically the Chinese hold a better position than the Soviet Union. Therefore, in the event of a leadership crisis, Kremlin may not be able to exercise 'Brezhnev Doctrine' in North Korea in view of the Chinese overall strategic superiority in the region. Rather the Chinese may like to exercise their own doctrine and mobilise forces to occupy North Korea, in response to Soviet actions in Hungary (1956), Czechoslovakia (1968) and recently in Afghanistan (1979). This needs not any further corroboration, as the Chinese have themselves confirmed it by walking into Vietnam in 1978.

From the view point of academic analysis, in the event of the son succeeding the father, the party leadership in the North may face a bitter civil war from within, since the long-standing dedicated service of senior party leaders at the centre may not be able to understand the concept of dynastic exercises within the framework of Marxism-Leninism. It is also possible that in the event of any single expression of factionalism among northern leaders, it may immediately involve China and the Soviet Union in a fresh conflict over their comparative supremacy over North Korea thus helping to foment a bitter 'class struggle' for supremacy among the leadership at higher echelons in North Korea.

The nature and extent of the rigorous and highly scientific propaganda, being carried out by the custodians of the International Communist Movement, by making fervent appeals to the people all over the world to rise in revolution, for the last several decades, evidently measures the nature and extent of the vacuum that exists beween the 'holy' scientific doctrine, when it was propounded in the nineteenth century and the 'realities of the situation' in the society that exists today. In any of the two contradictory systems, the ultimate survival of either of the two systems on conventional development process, short of nuclear war, will ultimately depend on the outcome, which is based fundamentally on the 'will' and 'aspirations' of the large majority of the people, and not on sporadic contractual outbursts of violence or dissatisfaction by an almost insignificant small section of the society, deriving inspiration some-times from across the border.

The question arises that in view of Chinese national priorities in the post-Mao period, what is its impact on the Korean conflict. The present North Korean leadership, which has been able somehow to establish a balance between Kremlin and Beijing, during the last three decades, has tried to stick to the Marxism-Leninism as the only course of the survival for the leadership. The Chinese, who are much pre-occupied with their modernisation crisis, can hardly speak of more than friendship 'cemented blood'. However, a stereo-typed regular strategic assistance from the Soviet Union to North Korea may continue in return for a reciprocal loyalty from the North Korean leaders in their comparatively friendlier attitude toward both the dearer one i.e. Soviet Union and the nearer one, i.e. China.

The oft-spoken massive Chinese people's presence in North Korea is the basic source of confidence to the Chinese as far as their intervention and hold on the North Korean affairs are concerned. The settling down of the Chinese 'volunteer' forces in North Korea, during the Korean War, led to the coming into power of some of the 'volunteers', who have gradually come up to central positions in the course of the last three decades.

Therefore, in view of the integrated character of impact of the Soviet and the Chinese governing forces in North Korea, the existence of the respective sympathisers among the top leadership cannot, in any case, be totally ruled out. It is difficult to find hard evidence in this respect in view of the totalitarian control and also due to the absence of freedom of expression and press in North Korea.

History shows that in none of the Kremlin protected States, except North Korea, a single leadership has been able to survive for more than three decades. Even in the Kremlin itself, there has been crisis of leadership and change has been witnessed. But the con-tinuance of a single leadership in North Korea stands in evidence that even in an event of crisis, it had been difficult to find out a second or a compromising candidate, who could have been unanimously approved by Moscow and Beijing.

However, the conflict on the the Korean peninsula evidences the most important example of a conflict where the political and strategic interests of three major powers clash in view of the United States and the Soviet Union balance v/s counterbalance in order to exercise due pressure in the mutual behavioural dynamism of the two Super Powers' policy planning and approaches.

In view of the changing patterns of political and strategic developments in North-East and East Asia, the identity of US-China interests in countering and combating the infiltrating and expanding character of the Soviet perceptions has more or less given a new orientation to this security complex zone in approaches, dimensions and perspective. Having the in-built implication of world peace, it has put forward manifold challenges for research, analysis and interpretation of the newly emerging framework of developing partnership in their foreign policy perspectives during the 1980s. The tension on the Korean peninsula, existing north and south of the 38th Parallel, can be reduced by peaceful approaches by the North and South of course with the inadvertent support and bonafide approval of the three major powers in view of their respective political and strategic interests.

Therefore, the interests of the three Major Powers, in the triangularity of their relationship, clash with each other. While the Chinese and US interests are identical in their common cause of containing the fast expanding and infiltrating designs of the Soviet Union on the one hand; on the other hand the Chinese and Soviet interests are identical in the continued survival of the North Korean regime and the ultimate communisation of the South—a policy which opposes fundamental US foreign policy interests. While there is a bitter rivalry between China and the Soviet Union, there is unanimity of opinion and identity in approach in the expulsion of US armed forces from South Korea, as pre-condition for a compromise formula like the much talked about concept of 'Federation'. In the support for North Korea, while the Soviet Union openly attacks 'US imperialism' and puts the condition of withdrawal of American forces by quoting North Korean dialects; China, of late, is often cautious in approach supporting the North Korean stand on the one hand but often careful on the matter of the withdrawal of American forces from South Korea, on the other hand. China is more inclined to maintain a status quo and prefers a tripartite international conference as a first step to the ultimate resolution of the conflict.

While all the three major powers, involved in the Korean conflict, view it in regional perspective, China alone seems to be more cautious lest a unified Korea, under the leadership of either of the two major Super Powers, should emerge as a vulnerable force on her border with the combined North-South Korean armies constituting the fourth place in the world. Both Soviet Union and China want to keep their position vulnerable in North Korea, possibly at the expense of the other.

In the triangularity of relationship, China feels somewhat safe since in the event of her political or strategic clash with the Soviet Union the United States may extend support, though limited one. Although the nature and extent of US support is difficult to determine, China banks on full US diplomatic support, partial political support and very limited sophisticated strategic support, against Soviet Union, strictly within the US foreign policy framework. The United States, on its own part, would never like the resolution of the Sino-Soviet conflict and would like to keep the present situation alive for decades. Thus, in the Korean context, China at least enjoys US diplomatic leverage vis-a-vis Soviet Union and may attempt to play it to the best of her advantage.

It is understood that China plays an important role and more appropriately holds an important leverage in conditioning the attitude and determining the approach of North Korea towards South Korea. Particularly on the unification issue, it is necessary to understand the Chinese interests in the Korean conflict and the tactics and cleverness involved in the modus operandi of its 'bargaining' in accordance with its own foreign policy interests. In this context the process of normalisation of Chinese relations with the United States, the mechanics involved in hard 'bargaining' and the ultimate compromise, have been earlier elucidated to enable us to understand how the Chinese pursue carefully and protect successfully their own interests with equally or probably better experienced hard bargainers.

In the final analysis, it can be said that to realise the cause of unification, concentrated and systematic efforts have to be made to create conditions under which the general desire for it can be given practical expression. In both the North and South, the solemn cause of national unification has been constantly used to win over the sentiments of the people and the pragmatic impact of the fear of an 'aggression' created in the masses has been helpful to continue in power. A state of constant emergency has worked on the social psychology of the people and led to increased production and prosperity in the South.

There is a basic difference in emphasis of the North and South, particularly regarding the modus operandi of their respective approaches to 'peaceful' unification. What is considered 'peaceful' by one is considered 'aggressive' by the other. South Korea contends that the goal of unification can be achieved gradually only 'step by step' in view of the deep mistrust and misunderstanding between the two. In view of the insecurity felt across the 38th parallel due to the threat of a possible attack from the North, South has been proposing a non-aggression treaty between Pyongyang and Seoul.

Although both have depended on negotiations, as has been apparent from the past, both have proceeded according to their own convenience and on their own terms and conditions, as has been discussed earlier. The South has termed the North's attitude as 'antagonistic' to 'peaceful unification', but the North has its own limitation and a set mathematical framework. Southern aspirations do not fit in that framework, thus causing a deadlock.

The North has not only to take care of its national considerations, but also take into account the compulsions of the International Communist Movement, which it considers as the most pious and religious doctrine. As such, any southern demand or 'peaceful' approach has to fit within the tenets of this doctrine, which is the most allergic virus for the southern leaders.

While the North demands the withdrawal of the American forces as a pre-requisite for any 'peaceful' resolution of the conflict, the South considers it as an in-built component for the survival of Korea as a nation.

While the North proposes a loose confederation of the two halves, and a joint conference of the representatives of political parties and social organisations of both the North and South, South considers this proposal ridiculous and treats it as an act of 'infiltration' and 'subversion' for the 'communisation' of the South.

As regards UN membership, the South favours entering the United Nations together with the North but as two sovereign independent nations like East Germany and West Germany. North rejects this, contending that such an event would be a de jure recognition of a permanent division and favours entry as a single entity under the name of the 'Republic of Koryo'. Although in theory it somehow sounds well but in practice it is in itself unworkable and impractical formula in view of the fact that vast ideological contradictions and differences of policy exist on various international conflicting situations and foreign policy issues. Both North and South have constantly reiterated that the cause of unification is basically an internal problem of the Korean people, but unfortunately two different sets of ideologies have been the main factor for the deadlock.

The question thus comes up to that what is the solution of this continued dilemma. Since both North and South have an ardent desire for 'peaceful' unification, there comes the vital question of the modus operandi of 'peaceful' approach. Since war has been universally decried as the means for lasting solution, the only option is to work out peace proposals jointly.

Thus a workable formula, at least to begin with, may be a meeting of the two Presidents, deliberating with open minds.

What is important, in this context, is that if the process is delayed with the passage of time and appearance of a new generation, which has never experienced life in a united Korea, the desire for unification may not be so intense as it is with the present leadership. The memories of the Korean War which are alive with the present generation, provoking enthusiasm for national unification, may become mere lessons of history for the upcoming generation.

# APPENDICES

## APPENDIX I

### SOUTH KOREA: AREA AND POPULATION

#### POPULATION (census results)

| Area* | October 1, 1966 | October 1, 1970 | October 1, 1975 | | |
|---|---|---|---|---|---|
| | | | Total | Male | Female |
| 98,859 sq. km.† | 29,192,726 | 31,465,654 | 34,678,972 | 17,445,246 | 17,233,726 |

* Excluding the demilitarized zone between North and South korea, with an area of 1,262 sq. km. (487 sq. miles.)
† 38,170 sq. miles. The figure indicates territory under the jurisdiction of the Republic of Korea on December 31st. 1977, surveyed on the basis of land register.

**Estimated Population** (mid-year): 35,860,000 in 1976; 36,436,000 in 1977; 37,019,000 in 1978; 37,605,000 in 1979.

#### ECONOMICALLY ACTIVE POPULATION* (1979 Average)

| | Males | Females | Total |
|---|---|---|---|
| Agriculture, forestry and fishing | 2,709,000 | 2,178,000 | 4,887,000 |
| Mining and quarrying | 102,000 | 9,000 | 111,000 |
| Manufacturing | 1,888,000 | 1,238,000 | 3,126,000 |
| Construction | 722,000 | 64,000 | 836,000 |
| Services | 2,938,000 | 1,766,000 | 4,704,000 |
| TOTAL IN EMPLOYMENT | 8,409,000 | 5,255,000 | 13,664,000 |
| Unemployed | 111,000 | 131,000 | 542,000 |
| TOTAL LABOUR FORCE | 8,820,000 | 5,386,000 | 14,206,000 |

* Excluding armed forces.

## APPENDIX II
### NORTH KOREA: AREA AND POPULATION

| Area* | Population | | | | | |
|---|---|---|---|---|---|---|
| | Official Estimates ‡ | | UN Estimates (mid-year) | | | |
| | Dec. 31, 1960 | Oct. 1, 1963 | 1976 | 1977 | 1978 | 1979 |
| 120,538 sq. km.† | 10,789,000 | 11,568,000 | 16,255,000 | 16,661,000 | 17,072,000 | 17,489,000 |

* Excluding the demilitarized zone between North and South Korea, with an area of 1,262 square kilometres (487 square miles).

† 46,540 square miles.

‡ *Source:* Institute of Economics of the World Socialist System, Moscow.

### LABOUR FORCE
(ILO estimates, '000 persons at mid-year)

| | 1950 | | | 1970 | | |
|---|---|---|---|---|---|---|
| | Males | Females | Total | Males | Females | Total |
| Agriculture, etc. | 1,334 | 1,620 | 2,954 | 1,483 | 1,794 | 3,278 |
| Industry | 705 | 405 | 1,110 | 1,073 | 584 | 1,657 |
| Services | 478 | 225 | 703 | 683 | 375 | 1,058 |
| TOTAL | 2,517 | 2,250 | 4,767 | 3,239 | 2,753 | 5,993 |

*Source:* ILO. *Labour Force Estimates and Projections, 1950–2000.*

**Mid-1978** (estimates in '000) : Agriculture etc. 3,606; Total 7,579 (*Source:* FAO. *Production Yearbook*).

## APPENDIX III
## NORTH-SOUTH COMPARISON

| | Unit | South Korea | North Korea |
|---|---|---|---|
| Population | person | 38,190,000 | 17,690,000 |
| GNP | $ | 57,600 mil | 13,000 mil |
| Per Capital GNP | $ | 1,508 | 750 |
| Exports | $ mil | 17,500 | 1,600 |
| Imports | $ mil | 22,200 | 1,700 |
| Electricity Output (Annual) | Kw/H | 35,600 mil | 21,600 mil |
| Automobile Production Capacity | Unit | 280,000 | 15,000 |
| Ships | Ton | 4,860,000 | 320,000 |
| Express Ways | Km | 1,255 | 240 |
| Telephone Lines | Line | 2,380,000 | 300,000 |

*Source: The Korean Herald, January 14, 1981, page 2.*

# FOOTNOTES

## Chapter I

1. Ho-min Yang, *North Korean Communism—A Comparative Analysis,* C.S. Chung and G.C. Kim, Eds., R.C.P.U., Seoul, 1980, page 195.
2. *Ibid.,* page 196.
3. *Ibid.*
4. Walker, Richard L., "Korean Unification; The Functional Approach—What Prospect," *Korea Observer,* Winter 1980, Seoul, page 384.
5. Sung-chul Yang, "The Kim Il Sung Cult in North Korea," *Korea and World Affairs,* Spring 1980, R.C.P.U., page 166.
6. *Ibid.*
7. Kim Il Sung, *Selected Works,* Vol. II, page 68.

## Chapter II

8. Oliver Robert, T., *Korea: Forgotten Nation* (Washington D.C., Public Affairs Press, 1944).
9. Anthony Eden, *Memoirs of Anthony Eden: The Reckoning* (Boston: Houghton-Mifflin Co., 1965), page 438; Cordell Hull, *Memoirs* (2 Vols, New York, Macmillan Co., 1948).
10. *Documents on American Foreign Relations,* Vol. VIII, July 1, 1945–December 31, 1946. World Peace Foundation, Princeton University Press, 1948, page 834.
11. *Korea's Quest for Peaceful Unification, Its History and Prospects for the Future,* Research Centre for Peace and Unification, Seoul, Korea, 1978, pages 21–22.
12. Yang Sung Chul, "The Kim Il Sung Cult in North Korea," *Korea and World Affairs,* Spring 1980, page 168.
13. *Korea's Quest for Peaceful Unification, Its History and Prospects for the Future,* Research Centre for Peace and Unification, Seoul, Korea.

**Chapter III**

14. Kim Chom Kon, *The Korean War, 1950–53,* Seoul, 1973, page 291.

15. Statement by the ROK Government on Its Determination to Achieve the Unification of Korea, May 28, 1951, in Royal Institute of International Affairs. Documents, 1951, page 632.

16. *New York Times,* June 26, 1951.

17. F.B.I.S., Daily Report, July 2, 1951, Korea, EEE 1.

18. UNCURK said that, for the time being, it was going on the assumption that there was no immediate need to concern itself with the five-point program, *New York Times,* July 1, 1951.

19. F.B.I.S., Daily Report, July 11, 1951, Korea, EEE 1.

20. *New York Times,* June 28, 1951.

21. *Ibid.*

22. F.B.I.S., Daily Report, July 11, 1951, Korea, EEE 2–3.

23. *Ibid.*

24. *Ibid.*

25. *Ibid.*

**Chapter IV**

26. Hinton, Harold C., "Sino-Soviet Relations and the Korean Question", in *Major Powers and Peace in Korea,* R.C.P.U., Seoul, 1979.

27. Chu Chi-hung, "The Struggle between Communist China, Soviet Russia and Pacific Community," in *The Korean Journal of International Studies,* Winter 1980–81, pages 83–84.

28. Dougherty, James E., and Phallzgraff, Jr., Robert L., *Contemporary Theories of International Relations,* Philadelphia, 1971, pages 257–258.

29. Halpern, A.M., "China's Foreign Policy Since the Cultural Revolution" in Mac-Farquhar (Ed.), *Sino-American Relations,* page 24.

30. See my concept of conflict termed 'Dialectic Diplomacy' in my book *Soviet Intervention in Afghanistan,* Ess Ess Publications, New Delhi, 1980, page XII.

31. Moscow Radio, May 11, 1977.

32. *Ibid.*

33. Shimizu Hayao, "Soviet Strategy in East Asia," *The Korean Journal of International Studies,* Winter 1980, page 72.

34. *Ibid.*

35. Scalapino, Robert A., "Communist Attitudes towards Korean Unification." *Korea Observer,* Winter 1980, page 357.

36. *Ibid.* In writing this part, I am greatly helped by the writings of Professor Scalapino, Robert A., *op. cit.*

37 Captain A.S. Krylink and Colonel V. Nogornyy, "Impression Military Journalists", *Krasnaya Zvezda,* Moscow, August 15, 1980, in Daily Report—Soviet Union, Foreign Broadcasting Information Service, August 19, 1980, C2–3; quoted by Robert A. Scalapino, *op. cit.,* page 358.

38. V. Vinogrador, 'Supporting a Just Cause', *Krasnaya Zvezda,* June 25, 1980, page 3

39. *Ibid.,* C2, quoted by Scalapino, *op. cit.,* page 358.

40. Scalapino, Robert A., *op. cit.,* page 358.

41. Mihaylov Commentary, September 9, 1980, in F.B.I.S., September 12, 1980, ci.; quoted by Scalapino, *op. cit.*

42. Scalapino, Robert A., *op. cit.,* page 359.

43. Izvestia, "Peaceful DPR-ROK Dialogue Undermined", April 16, 1980, quoted by Scalapino. *op. cit.,* page 359.

44. Nikoloy Klokhlov Commentary, F.B.I.S., June 26, 1980, Scalapino, *op. cit,* page 360.

45. Scalapino, *op. cit.,* page 361.

46. Pyongyang, KCNA, September 1, 1980, quoted by Scalapino, *op. cit.,* page 367.

47. For a detailed and exhaustive analysis of Soviet Intervention in Afghanistan, see my book *Soviet Intervention in Afghanistan,* published in March 1980 from New Delhi.

**Chapter V**

48. Hak Joon Kim, *The Unification Policy of South and North Korea,* Seoul National University Press, 1977 page 69.

49. *Ibid.*

50. *Ibid.*

51. UN Document, A/AC, 26/9.

52. Glenn, D. Paige, "Korea," in Cyrid E. Black and Thomas P. Thornton (Eds.), *Communism and Revolution* (Princeton: Princeton University Press, 1964), pp. 230–231.

53. Bong Baik, *Kim Il Sung: Biography* (Tokyo: Miraisha, 1969), III, page 472

54. Hak Joon Kim, *The Unification Policy of South and North Korea,* Seoul National University Press, page 175.

55. *Nodong Sinmun,* May 5, 1960, quoted by Prof. Hak Joon Kim, *The Unification Policy of South and North Korea,* Seoul National University Press, page 176.

56. Yong Soon Yim, "A Comparative Study of Foreign Policy: The Case of Two Koreas," *Journal of Korean Affairs,* Vol. V, No. 4 (January, 1976), pages 6–7.

57. Han-Been Lee, *Korea: Time, Change, and Administration* (Honolulu: East-West Center Press, 1968), Chapter 6.

58. Han Sung Joo, "Political Dissent in South Korea, 1948–1961," in Kim Se-Jin and Cho Chang-Hyon (Eds.), *Government and Politics of Korea,* Silver Spring, Md.: Research Institute on Korean Affairs, 1972, pp. 43–69.

59. ROK Foreign Ministry, *Tongil Munje Yongu,* pp. 324–325, quoted by Hak Joon Kim, *The Unification Policy of South and North Korea,* Seoul National University Press, page 183.

60. North Korean 'Federation' proposal has been discussed later in detail.

61. Hak Joon Kim, *The Unification Policy of South and North Korea,* Seoul National University Press, 1977, page 188.

62. *Peking Review,* Vol. IV, No. 28, July 14, 1961, pp. 5–7.

63. Kim Nam-Sik, *North Korean Strategy against ROK: Korean Frontier,* Vol. I, No. 8, Oct. 1970, pages 18–23.

64. *Selected Writings of Kim Il Sung,* Revolutionary Publishers, 1971, page 105.

65. The Comprehensive Report on the Task of the Central Committee to Fourth Congress of the KWP, Pyongyang, 1961, page 106.

66. *Kim Il Sung,* Biography, Vol. III, page 474

67. *Selected Writings of Kim IL Sung,* Revolutionary Publishers, 1971, page 109.

68. *Ibid.,* pages 464–466.

69. *Ibid.,* page 468.

70. Scalapino, Robert A. (Ed.) ,*North Korea Today,* Praeger, New York, 1963, page 50.

71. Seung Hee Kim, *Foreign Capital for Economic Development: A Korean Case Study* (New York: Praeger Publishers, 1970).

72. Park Chung Hee, *Selected Speeches and Interviews: Towards Peaceful Unification,* Second Edition, Seoul, Korea, 1978.

73. KCNA, February 15, 1972, in FBIS Daily Report, February 17, 1972, North Korea.

74. Young Whan Kihl, "Korean Response to Major Rapproachement," in Young C. Kim (Ed.), *Major Powers and Korea* (Silver Spring, Md.: Research Institute on Korean Affairs, 1973) pp. 151–154.

75. *Korea Past and Present,* Kwangmyong Publishing Co., Seoul, Korea, First Edition, 1972, page 136.

76. Park Chung Hee, *Towards Peaceful Unification,* 1978, pages 84–85.

77. *New York Times,* June 24, 1973, 2 : 3.

78. Park Chung Hee, *Towards Peaceful Unification,* 1978, Seoul, Korea, pages 97–98.
    "Once such an agreement is concluded, the South and North can coexist peacefully until the time of national unification, during which period they can consolidate the foundations of unification one by one through active dialogue, exchanges and cooperation. This is consonant with the spirit of the June 23 foreign policy statement made by the Government last summer. We clearly understand that no matter how ardently we long for unification, unification cannot be realised in a day or two. Since this is no time to take up the unification issue forthwith, nor can we expect an atmosphere ripe for national unification, in view of the present relations between the South and the North, we must continue, during which period we can, as I have already stated, consolidate the foundations for national unification step by step. This is the very spirit of the June 23 statement and, at the same time, is our just proposal."

79. *New York Times,* March 26, 1974, 9 : 1.

80. President Park Chung Hee, *Towards Peaceful Unification,* Seoul, Korea, 1978, page 137.

81. Shin Bum Shik (Ed.), *Major Speeches by Korea's Park Chung Hee,* Seoul Hollym Corporation, 1970, page 60.

82. *Ibid.,* page 257.

83. Details of North-South economic conditions are clear from the labels at Appendices at the end.

84. *Nodon Sinmun,* May 5, 1960, *op. cit.*

85. Walker, Richard L., "Korean Unification—Functional Approach —What Prospects," in *Korea Observer,* Winter 1980, page 374.

86. *Ibid.*

87. *Korea Herald,* January 13, 1981, page 1. For a full text of President Chun Doo Hwan's proposals, see *ibid.,* page 5.

88. *Ibid.*

89. *Ibid.,* page 5.

90. *Ibid.*

91. *Ibid.*

92. *Ibid.,* page 1.